WHY BE DIFFERENT?

A Look Into Judaism

BY JANICE PRAGER AND ARLENE LEPOFF

Illustrated by Peter Kuper

BEHRMAN HOUSE, INC.
West Orange, New Jersey

Copyright 1986 by Janice Prager and Arlene Lepoff
Published by Behrman House, Inc.
235 Watchung Avenue
West Orange, NJ 07052

Manufactured in the United States of America

ISBN 0-87441-427-X

TO DENNIS PRAGER

*Who is making the case for
Judaism in our time and who inspired us
to write this book*

Preface

For Jews living in freedom, the greatest Jewish problem is not antisemitism. It is the large number of Jews who are alienated from Judaism and the Jewish people. And the major reason for this alienation is terribly simple. Most Jews are given little, if any, reason to be Jewish.

Jewish life is overwhelmingly preoccupied with *how* to survive—how to combat antisemitism, how to help poor and persecuted Jews, how to keep Israel safe—and *how* to be Jewish—how to observe the holidays, how to pray, how to chant the Bar-Mitzvah portion. All of these are of course crucial to Jewish life and to Jewish survival. But there is a far more important question that Jews need answered first. *Why* should the Jews survive, *why* in a free society with so many fine and kind non-Jews, should one be Jewish? Why, in short, should one be different? Only when taught the *whys* will most Jews care about the *hows*.

When Jews receive a rational and convincing answer to this question, they will have reasons to remain Jews and lead lives committed to Judaism's values. That is the purpose of this book. Its aim is to intellectually prepare young Jews to deal with the powerful challenges to their Jewishness that will inevitably confront them in high school and college.

The overwhelming emphasis on *why* is not the only distinguishing feature of *Why Be Different?* A second distinguishing feature is the emphasis on Judaism's challenges and demands. As a result, the student may not always feel entirely comfortable. But neither the Torah, nor the Prophets, nor the Rabbis sought primarily to comfort Jews. Using their model, then, we sought to challenge and uplift the student to Judaism's moral and religious values.

Yet a third characteristic—*Why Be Different?* is designed as much for parental teaching of Judaism as for classroom work. We take seriously the injunction to parents to teach their children Judaism and character. Throughout the writing of our book, we have envisioned parents discussing its ideas with their children.

Finally, *Why Be Different?* has been enriched by years of testing with students in an actual classroom setting. It incorporates their comments and suggestions, as well as those of their teachers and many other Jewish educators.

Space limitations prevent our listing all the Jewish educators who have given of their expertise and time. In many ways *Why Be Different?* is our way of saying thank you to them and to the many other unheralded conveyors of the Jewish tradition.

We do, however, want to thank Rabbi Yitz Greenberg, Dr. David Elcott, Dr. David Kraemer, Rabbi Nachum Braverman, and Mr. Leonid Feldman. These distinguished educators were our readers and critics. They were extraordinarily generous, patient, and helpful—but they should not be held accountable for what finally was written. We are also profoundly grateful to Dr. Sheldon Dorph and Rabbi Phil Warmflash who gave unstintingly of their wisdom and experience and who, along with the students and teachers of the Los Angeles Hebrew High School, enabled us to test and improve our materials continuously.

We warmly acknowledge Professors Emil Fackenheim and Elie Wiesel whose insights are cited in Chapter 3, Rabbi Harold Kushner whose ideas we cite in Chapters 4 and 15, and Avital Shcharansky's *Next Year in Jerusalem* from which the story in Chapter 18 is retold.

We are deeply indebted to Joseph Telushkin, coauthor with Dennis Prager of *The Nine Questions People Ask About Judaism* and *Why The Jews? The Reason For Antisemitism*, two books that have profoundly affected the way in which Judaism is taught. His support, insights, encouragement, and most of all his Jewish teachings were instrumental to the writing of *Why Be Different?* We miss Joseph deeply, but our loss was Israel's gain.

Mr. Nick Mandelkern at Behrman House deserves great praise for his superb editing—and for his equally impressive qualities of patience. All authors should be blessed with such a sympathetic yet critical editor.

We would also like to bless David Prager who pulled the plug on our computer only one time, and who usually played quietly with his fleet of buses during the long months of writing this book.

Aharon, aharon haviv, there are no words to describe our loving gratitude to Dennis Prager. His uniquely effective way of conveying Judaism to adults was our model in writing this book for young people. His talks and his writings, his endless hours of editing and discussions with us, and his moral passion kept us going through our most difficult moments. He made this book possible.

Janice Prager and Arlene Lepoff
Los Angeles and New York, 1986

Contents

INTRODUCTION

Who Are the Jews?

CHAPTER
1

Chaos in Krime City

In a distant corner of the planet, there was a city so bad that even its own inhabitants called it Krime City. Tiny but terrible, Krime City never had any contact with the outside world. The people within its borders lied, cheated, stole from each other, even attacked and killed each other—the people would do anything to get what they wanted. "Survival of the strongest" was the law of the land.

One day a team of explorers from a far-away kingdom happened to discover the chaotic city. They were shot at as soon as they approached the city walls. As bullets whizzed by them and bounced off their bullet-proof exploration suits, they called a hasty retreat. The explorers returned home to describe their discovery to their king.

The king was extremely disturbed by their report. "I'm glad that you have discovered an isolated city," he told them, "but I don't like the way the people behave there. I must find a way to transform that terrible city into a good one and its people into better people."

For forty days and nights, the king thought about the problem. Finally he came up with a solution. He created a set of laws for the townspeople to follow. But how would he get the unruly residents of Krime City to follow his laws? The king decided he would start with just one family. If one family accepted the laws and began to live by them, they would set an example for the other families to follow.

A messenger was sent to Krime City to find a family to accept this task. He traveled in an armored truck with an indestructible loudspeaker on its roof. Throughout Krime City, on every street corner and public square, he repeated the king's question:

"Will your family accept this responsibility?"

Finally, after being rejected by many families, the messenger found one, the Swej family, to accept the responsibility. The Swej family agreed to learn the king's rules, to live by them, and to teach them to all the other families of the city. The messenger warned them:

"Because you are accepting this obligation, you will have a difficult time. Other families will dislike you. And remember, improvement of this city and its people will take a very long time, maybe even centuries. It will certainly be many generations before everyone accepts the king's authority and his laws."

In spite of the immense difficulty of this responsibility, the Swej family chose to accept it.

QUESTIONS FOR DISCUSSION
- *What is your opinion of the family that chose to accept this obligation?*
- *What might be the consequences of their decision?*
- *What would you have done if you were approached by the king's messenger? Why?*

Who are the Jews?

The Jews are the descendants of Abraham, Isaac, and Jacob; and Sarah, Rebecca, Rachel and Leah. Approximately 3,500 years ago, the Jews lived in Egypt and were enslaved by the ruling Pharoahs. They remained enslaved for hundreds of years. Then, led by Moses, they escaped from Egypt and spent forty years wandering in the Sinai Desert. At Mount Sinai something happened that made the Jews different from all the other peoples of the world.

At Sinai, God chose the Jews for a special role in the world. They had to live according to God's laws as found in the Torah, become an example to the rest of the world, and bring the belief in one God to the world. By accepting these responsibilities, the Jews became the Chosen People. The task given to them by God was to live according to the Torah's values and code of laws, thereby teaching all of humanity about God, how to become better people, and how to make a better world.

The Jews had just escaped from slavery. They had traveled by day and by night, with the Egyptian armies close behind them. They were exhausted and worried about the future. What made them decide to accept the task that God presented to them? Why should they have taken upon themselves such a tremendous responsibility? Perhaps all the miracles that God performed when taking the Jews out of Egypt, and all the miracles at Mount Sinai, convinced them. Or perhaps the Jews at Sinai understood that what God wanted them to do was the right thing to do.

Whatever the reason, the Jews did accept God's challenge to live by special rules and work to perfect the world. Ever since, they have been called the Chosen People.

Why the Jews?

Why did God choose the Jews for this difficult task? Jewish tradition gives three possible explanations: The first explanation is that the Jews were chosen because their ancestor, Abraham, was the first person to recognize and accept one God. A second explanation says that God offered the Torah to several other nations before offering it to the Jews. They all refused, however, because they did not want to accept such a tremendous responsibility. A third explanation is that the Jews were chosen because they were neither strong, nor rich, nor influential. God chose them so that any success they achieved in changing the world would be due to God and the Torah, and not their own powers.

The Jews are called the Chosen People. This means that they have special responsibilities and obligations. It does not mean that the Jews are superior to other people.

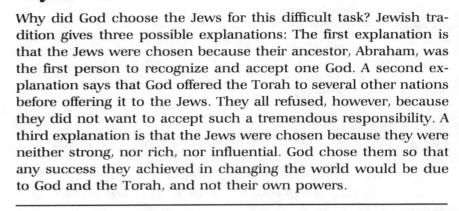

One God: a revolutionary idea

The Jews were chosen for a difficult task: to teach the world that there is only one God. At that time, few people could accept such a teaching. In the ancient world, the idea of one God was a completely new and strange concept. Nations that lived around the Jews, in fact all the peoples of the world, worshiped their own gods. Their gods were stone idols, trees, stars, rocks, and rivers. People chose gods according to their needs. When it was too dry, they prayed to a god of rain; when it was too wet, they prayed to a sun god. Tribes believed that their gods were with them as they went into battle. If they lost a war, they abandoned their own gods in favor of the gods of the enemy.

In teaching the world that there is only one God, the Jews presented a completely new and revolutionary idea. They were the first people to understand that there is only one God, the same God for all people and all nations, the creator of everything in the universe. This idea is called **monotheism**. "Mono" means one, and "theism" means the belief in God. The Jews were the first people in history to believe in monotheism.

Ethical monotheism

The Jews brought to the world another idea, even more important and more revolutionary than monotheism. This was **ethical monotheism**. Ethical monotheism is the idea that God demands that all people be good. God requires ethical (good) behavior from every human being.

Ethical monotheism means there is only one final authority for everyone in the world, and that authority is God. According to the teachings of Judaism, God is a higher authority than any human being or group of human beings—higher than any leader, government, or army. God's ethical laws and standards apply to everyone. Ethical monotheism is the most important idea in history, and is the key to making the world good.

Ethical monotheism was introduced to the world by the Jewish people.

The Jewish role in the world

The Jews were chosen by God to play a special role in the world. Their task is to teach people about God and to make the world a better place. There are two ways that Jews are to work at this task:

1. By spreading the idea of ethical monotheism throughout the world.

2. By living according to the Torah. By doing this, Jews will become an example to the rest of the world. As the great Jewish prophet Isaiah said, the Jews must become "a light to the nations."

It may seem that the Jewish task is impossible. After all, the Jews have never been more than a tiny percentage of the world's population. How could such a small group reach the other nations with its message? And yet, throughout more than 3,000 years of their history, the Jews have managed to influence many other societies and religions with their ethical system and belief in one God.

Every single Jew is responsible for this difficult task. You may wonder how one person can make a difference. You may ask, "How can I, by myself, make the world a better place?"

Ethics of the Fathers, a book written more than 1,800 years ago, gives a good answer to this question. It states: "It is not up to you to finish the task, but you are not free to abandon it."

It is understood that you, alone, will not accomplish this task of perfecting the world. But by leading a Jewish life, you—along with millions of other Jews—will make a difference. If even half of the Jews in the world today lived by Judaism's laws and values, the effect on the world would be enormous. Just imagine the situation that would be created if every Jew conducted his life with the goal of making a better world through Judaism. The impact on society would be staggering and an ethical revolution would take place!

Making the world a better place is a central goal of Judaism.

PART ONE

Why We Need God

Beyond the Planet of the Apes

The Starship Quest is on a mission —to explore unknown planets in faraway solar systems. The next stop is the Planet Chance, in the Coincidental Solar System.

In the spaceship, Captain Doubt and Captain Certain are preparing the crew for landing. The captains tell the crew members that when the spaceship reaches the planet surface, they are to stay inside the ship until they receive further orders.

As the ship touches down, the captains prepare to move onto the unfamiliar terrain.

"What's that noise?" asks Captain Doubt as the hatch door swings open.

Captain Certain follows him outside. They are both too amazed to speak. In every direction they see monkeys, hundreds of monkeys, in all shapes and sizes. Even more astounding, there are also hundreds of electric typewriters scattered every few feet. The monkeys appear to be fascinated with the typewriters and are jumping up and down on the keys.

As the captains move closer, they see a seemingly endless roll of typed material coming out of each typewriter. They continue to walk and are amazed to see that there are in fact thousands of monkeys and thousands of typewriters. In a fervor, the two captains race back to the Starship Quest and immediately summon their two hundred crew members. They deliver the following directive:

"Go out and read the material coming out of each typewriter. If you find something intelligible, bring it back here immediately."

Months go by and no one reports back to the ship. One day, almost a year later, an excited crew member, Lt. Eureka, comes stumbling into the captains' quarters, carrying a huge pile of paper.

"Look, Look! I found it! I found the Encyclopedia Britannica, Volume 6, coming out of one of the typewriters. I verified it on my wrist computer library scanner."

The captains examine the material in Lt. Eureka's hands, and sure enough, it is the Encyclopedia Britannica, Volume 6. Captain Certain proclaims:

"There must be a higher form of intelligence somewhere on this planet for this to have happened."

"Don't be ridiculous!" yells Captain Doubt. "It's just a coincidence."

"What do you mean a coincidence?" asks Captain Certain. "This could not occur just by chance."

"Of course it could," insists Captain Doubt. "If you let enough monkeys pound on enough typewriters for enough years, you can get the Encyclopedia Britannica, Volume 6."

QUESTIONS FOR DISCUSSION
• If the monkeys were given enough time, do you think that they would eventually type Treasure Island? What about the New York telephone directory? How about a list of the National League Baseball Teams?
• Can these things happen by chance? Captain Doubt thinks so. Do you agree with him? Or does the opinion of Captain Certain make more sense?

Does God exist?

The argument between Captain Certain and Captain Doubt represents the age-old argument about God's existence: Is there a designer and creator of the universe, or is everything the result of chance? Another way of asking this question is: Did God create the world or did everything come about by coincidence?

Captain Doubt and Captain Certain each represent opposite positions in this old debate about God. Captain Doubt takes the position of an **atheist**, someone who does not believe God exists. Captain Doubt believes that the Encyclopedia Britannica, Volume Six, came about by chance, not by design. In the same way, an atheist believes that everything in the universe came about by chance, not by God's design. Captain Certain represents a **theist** or someone who does believe in the existence of God. The theist does not believe that everything came about by chance.

People have been debating the existence of God ever since the Jews introduced the knowledge of God to the world. The debate will go on, because unlike other questions, this one cannot be answered using scientific methods. When you study math, for example, you can usually offer proof to justify your answers. For the question of God's existence, however, proof is not as easy to find.

Does the universe have a design and a designer?

The atheist recognizes that there is design in the universe, but he does not believe that there is a designer. He believes that the design in the universe came about because of the chance interaction between matter and energy. An atheist believes that it is ultimately by chance that cows give milk, trees bear fruit, and people think. These designs, he argues, came about by sheer coincidence and were not designed by anyone.

The theist believes that the world's incredibly intelligent design had to have an intelligent designer—God. How could the unbelievably complex workings of a single cell, let alone the human brain, come about just by chance? The theist argues that it is more logical to believe in God than in chance. The theist might tell this story to support his position:

You are walking in the wilderness after a tremendous rock slide. Suddenly you stumble upon a group of rocks that spell out HELLO. You think to yourself, "Wow! What a coincidence!"

You keep hiking and just fifty feet later, you see another HELLO spelled out by some rocks. You begin to suspect that someone has arranged those rocks.

When you see a third HELLO, you are certain that a designer is at work. These rock arrangements would not occur by chance.

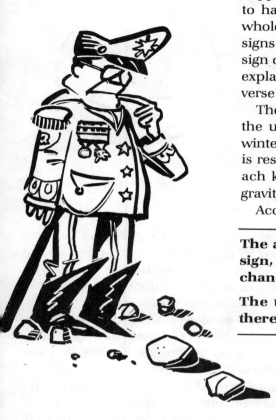

The design of the rocks into the word HELLO could not have happened by chance. It had to have a designer. Now if HELLO had to have a designer, doesn't the far more complex design of the whole universe have to have a designer? Could the billions of designs of the world, from the universe's laws of physics to the design of one molecule, really have happened by chance? The theist explains that if HELLO had to have a designer, so did the universe.

The theist can offer endless examples of God as the designer of the universe. How do birds know to fly to warm climates every winter? Who placed the colors of the rainbow in their order? Who is responsible for the miracle of childbirth? How does your stomach know exactly how to digest its food? Who made sure that gravity would prevent the earth from just flying away?

According to theists, the answer in all these cases is God.

The atheist believes that even though the universe has a design, it does not have a designer. Everything came about by chance.

The theist believes that the universe's design means that there is a designer—God.

How is it possible to believe in something that can't be seen?

The atheist uses this question to argue that God does not exist. Atheists believe that only things that can be scientifically proven really exist. Therefore, since we cannot see, hear, touch, taste, smell, or measure God, God does not exist.

The theist is not troubled at all by this question. There are very many things in life that everyone knows exist but which are not scientifically provable. Friendship and love are two such examples. When your best friend is out of town, does your friendship still exist? Does it exist even though you can't see it, or touch it, or measure it? How do you know that friendship exists? What about the love your parents have for you? Can you hold it in your hand? Can you scientifically prove or measure it? How do you know love exists?

Like love and friendship, people know God exists, even though they cannot prove it in scientific ways.

People can know that God exists. But because God is not physical, they cannot scientifically prove that God exists.

God cannot be reached through people's physical senses alone. God must be found in other ways.

Facing the Sun

Chaim was a very rich man who had traveled all over the world. He had fulfilled all of his desires except for one. He wanted to see God to prove for himself that God exists. The thought that he would die before seeing God troubled him greatly.

One day, he approached his rabbi and said:

"Rabbi, I want to see God. Why should I believe in God if I can't see Him? If God really exists, why doesn't He show Himself to me?"

"Well, Chaim," answered the rabbi, "before you can see God, you must look into the face of the sun."

Chaim dashed outside and turned his face up towards the bright sun. But the powerful light immediately blinded him, and he had to turn away. He returned to the rabbi and exclaimed, "Rabbi, what are you trying to do to me? I can't look at the sun. It's so bright that it hurts my eyes."

The rabbi answered Chaim with a question:

"How can you, a mere human who cannot even face the sun, which is only one of God's creations, expect to come face-to-face with God, Himself?"

QUESTIONS FOR DISCUSSION
- *What lesson was the rabbi trying to teach Chaim?*
- *Was Chaim wrong to question his belief in God?*
- *If someone came to you with a question like Chaim's, how would you answer it?*

Why can't people see God?

What does God look like? Is God an old man with a long beard, sitting on a golden throne?

Of course not. God is not physical and therefore cannot be described in physical terms. The only things humans can describe in physical terms are the things that God created. And as the rabbi in the story showed Chaim, often people cannot even look at the things God created. So how can people ever expect to look at God?

Judaism also teaches that God is infinite, invisible, and not physical. And therefore Judaism says that it is wrong to try to make a physical image of God. The moment you make a physical image of God, you are limiting what God is, in your own mind. This is why Jews are not allowed to create any pictures of God. So, for example, you will never see a painting or a statue of God in any synagogue or temple. As one famous Jewish philosopher wrote, "Nothing we can possibly imagine can resemble God, who made us. It is impossible for us to picture God as He must be."

How does Judaism describe God?

The only way people can think about anything is in human terms. That is all right for most things. But when a person tries to think about God in human terms, his thinking is limited by the fact that God is way beyond what humans can understand. Therefore, when Jews try to understand and know God, they should not try to do so by describing God's appearance. They should, however, try to know two things: What are God's qualities and what does God want from them?

God's Qualities

1. *God is perfect*. Jewish writings describe God as kind, compassionate, just and merciful. God is all good. In fact, God is perfect.

2. *God is the source of good and evil*. God has given people a conscience and moral rules. Moral rules tell people the difference between good and evil. "God is the source of good and evil" means that God and God's laws tell people what is right and what is wrong.

3. *God is supernatural*. This means that God is completely above and beyond nature. God is not the same as nature, and God is not in nature. God created the sky, but is not the sky, nor in the sky. The same is true for the ocean, the trees, the sun, and even all of nature. All these and all of nature are merely creations of God. God is above them and above all of nature.

As Chaim discovered in the story, God is so powerful that just one of God's creations can overwhelm a person. How much greater, then, must be God, who created all of nature.

4. *God is personal*. God is not just the creator of the world or some great "force." God is someone you can relate to. God has a

personal relationship with every human being. God knows you, God understands you, and God cares about you. Knowing that God has a personal relationship with you enables you to feel God's persence in your everyday life. Judaism is based on the relationship individuals have with an understanding, loving God.

5. *God is holy*. One of the most widely used Jewish descriptions of God is that God is "The Holy One." Holy means the highest and the most special. There are many holy things in the world, and all holiness comes from God.

What God expects from Jews

Once a Jew understands God's qualities, it becomes much clearer what God expects.

1. *Adopt God's qualities*. God is kind, compassionate, just and merciful, so Jews should be all those things as well. God is the ideal towards which people should strive.

2. *Be good*. The most important thing that God expects from people is to do good things for fellow human beings. God, the source of good, demands that people do good. The most famous and most important statement in the Torah is "Love your neighbor as your self, I am God."

3. *Worship God, not nature*. All over the ancient world, people always worshiped things in nature. But Judaism challenged human thinking when it said that God created nature and that only God may be worshipped. Even today, some people think everything—from childbirth to a beautiful sunrise—comes from nature and not from God. Judaism demands that people worship only God and not nature.

4. *Love God*. Judaism teaches that God loves all people, and that God chose the Jews out of love for them. Jews should try to love God. The more personal a Jew's relationship is with God, the more he will come to love God and appreciate all that God has done. In Jewish prayers, God is often referred to as a loving father, who also has loving motherly qualities. This teaches that Jews should not only obey God, they should also love God.

5. *Be holy*. While God demands that everyone be good, God has one other, extremely important demand of the Jewish people: "You shall be holy because I your God am holy." This commandment is in the Torah, and it means that Jews should live a life that is as special and as meaningful as possible.

Can a Jew Question his Belief in God?

Ideally, a Jew relates to God with love and appreciation. But sometimes things happen to people that cause them to question God, or even to question their belief in God. This might be called "struggling" with God. According to Judaism, it is acceptable to question and to struggle with God.

But it is not acceptable to ignore God. Even if a Jew goes as far as questioning God's existence, he must continue to try to find answers for himself. By struggling, thinking about God, discussing God with others, and most important, continuing to observe Judaism's laws, a Jew will eventually come to have a stronger and better relationship with God.

A Jew may love God or a Jew may question God, but a Jew may not ignore God.

CHAPTER 4

The Time Machine

Michelle's father had decided to redecorate his office. One Sunday he went downtown to the antique shops. He returned with a strange contraption, a little booth with dials and levers running up and down its sides. It was, he said, a time machine.

"That's what the dealer called it," he laughed. "Whatever it is, it'll be fun to have in my office." So he brought it home and stored it in the garage.

When Michelle saw the machine, she was intrigued by it. Something about the unusual antique excited her. She knew that her friend David would also be fascinated with it and so she invited him over.

The next afternoon, Michelle and David climbed inside the booth.

"Are you sure we should be doing this? What if this machine actually works?" asked David. Before Michelle could answer, the machine began vibrating. It felt as if they were hurtling through space.

"This is incredible!" David shouted into the roar of the machine. "I think we're really doing it, moving through time!"

Suddenly the machine seemed to slow down and finally touched ground. The walls of the booth dissolved into the air. Michelle and David were in the middle of massive destruction. The earth itself was shaking, toppling trees and buildings. Fires were erupting everywhere. People were screaming and running for cover to avoid being crushed or burned alive.

"Oh God! What happened? Where are we?" exclaimed David.

"I don't know where we are but we're in the middle of a terrible earthquake. Please David, let's get out of here. I can't stand seeing all of this suffering," yelled Michelle, as she frantically began to turn the dials that were in the panel box in front of her.

"Oh!—that was horrible," cried Michelle after they had taken off again. "People dying and suffering, and there was nothing anyone could do about it! Wait—we're slowing down. Oh, please, let us be home."

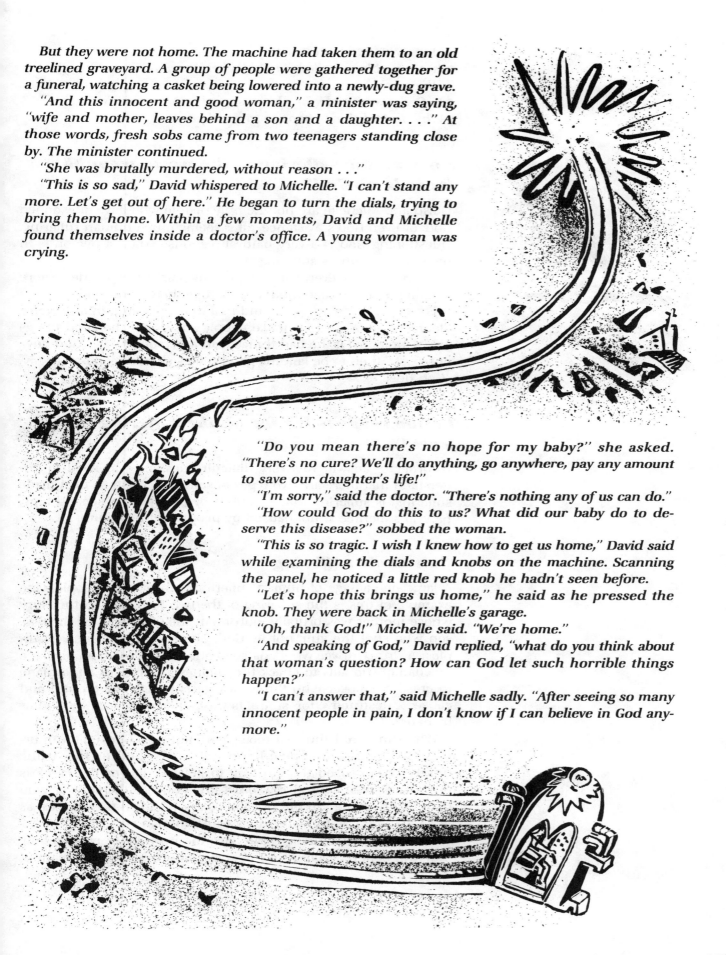

But they were not home. The machine had taken them to an old treelined graveyard. A group of people were gathered together for a funeral, watching a casket being lowered into a newly-dug grave.

"And this innocent and good woman," a minister was saying, "wife and mother, leaves behind a son and a daughter. . . ." At those words, fresh sobs came from two teenagers standing close by. The minister continued.

"She was brutally murdered, without reason . . ."

"This is so sad," David whispered to Michelle. "I can't stand any more. Let's get out of here." He began to turn the dials, trying to bring them home. Within a few moments, David and Michelle found themselves inside a doctor's office. A young woman was crying.

"Do you mean there's no hope for my baby?" she asked. "There's no cure? We'll do anything, go anywhere, pay any amount to save our daughter's life!"

"I'm sorry," said the doctor. "There's nothing any of us can do."

"How could God do this to us? What did our baby do to deserve this disease?" sobbed the woman.

"This is so tragic. I wish I knew how to get us home," David said while examining the dials and knobs on the machine. Scanning the panel, he noticed a little red knob he hadn't seen before.

"Let's hope this brings us home," he said as he pressed the knob. They were back in Michelle's garage.

"Oh, thank God!" Michelle said. "We're home."

"And speaking of God," David replied, "what do you think about that woman's question? How can God let such horrible things happen?"

"I can't answer that," said Michelle sadly. "After seeing so many innocent people in pain, I don't know if I can believe in God anymore."

● Is it possible to believe in God when there is so much suffering in the world?
● Is God responsible for all the suffering in the world?
● Why do bad things happen to good people?

Does all the suffering in the world mean that there is no God?

David and Michelle are not the only people who have questioned God, or even God's existence, after seeing much human suffering. Questioning God is a very natural response when a person is in pain, or sees others suffering.

There are, however, some important points to consider before deciding that because there is suffering, there is no God.

For one thing, both good and bad things happen in a person's lifetime. The bad things make people suffer, but the good things give people joy. If the bad things lead a person to say, "God does not exist," then to be fair, the good things should lead one to say, "God does exist."

Is God responsible for all the suffering in the world?

In order to answer this very difficult question, you need to understand that there are two types of suffering. The first, man-made suffering, is suffering that is caused by people. The second type, natural suffering, is not caused by people but by nature.

Man-made suffering

A large percentage of human suffering is caused by people. One example of this is the suffering of the two teenagers in the story whose mother was brutally murdered. She was killed by the person who shot the gun, not by God. There are many such examples: A drunk driver who kills someone on the road; an airplane mechanic who fails to check the engines and causes an airplane to crash; a smoker who throws a cigarette onto the ground and causes a destructive forest fire. Is this suffering caused by God or by people?

Who murdered the two teenagers' mother—God or the murderer? Who ran over people on the road—God or the drunk driver? Who caused the airplane to crash—God or the careless mechanic? Who caused the forest fire—God or the smoker who didn't care enough to put out the cigarette? In all these cases, as in so many more, human beings cause human suffering.

Judaism teaches that people have the freedom to choose how they will behave, even if they choose to hurt people. God cannot be blamed for the bad things people choose to do. This is true even for the Holocaust.

God did not make the Holocaust; people did. God did not build concentration camps or gas chambers; people did. The evil that the Nazis did must be blamed on the Nazis themselves. They freely chose to act as they did. And since people are free to do good or evil, man-made suffering should be blamed on people, not on God. God cannot be held responsible for man-made suffering, even suffering as horrible as the Holocaust.

Man-made suffering cannot be blamed on God because it is caused by people.

Natural suffering

The second kind of human suffering is not caused by people but by nature. The two most obvious examples are disease, such as when a child dies of cancer, and natural catastrophies, such as when an earthquake destroys a city. It is impossible to explain fully why God allows these things to happen. Even the most knowledgeable Jews cannot fully explain natural suffering.

Some people die of cancer and some people are miraculously cured; human beings cannot know why. Why does one person live, while another person dies? This is one of the most perplexing questions that people face. But even though we cannot fully understand natural suffering, Judaism does deal with this question and attempts to provide some explanations.

The story of Job

The Book of Job, found in the Bible, is Judaism's major work dealing with the challenging question: Why does God allow innocent people to suffer?

Job is a good and righteous man. He is faithful to God and to God's commandments. But suddenly one tragedy after another begins to strike him. All of his children are killed, and he develops an illness in which his body is covered with boils. He endures severe emotional and physical pain, and does not understand why God is causing him so much suffering.

Although he tries to maintain his faith in God, his suffering is unbearable and in desperation he cries out: "God! I want an answer. Why me? I have been a good and righteous man. I have tried to follow your commandments. I give charity to the poor. I've never taken anything that does not belong to me. I never boasted of my wealth. I challenge you, God, to tell me why I am suffering."

God comes to answer Job's questions about natural suffering. Out of a whirlwind, God speaks to Job:

Where were you when I planned the earth?
Tell me, if you are so wise . . . .
Were you there when I stopped the sea? . . .
Have you seen where the snow is stored? . . .
Do you give the horse its strength? . . .
Do you show the hawk how to fly?

God's answer is hard to understand because it does not talk about Job's suffering at all. Instead, God answers Job's question with another question: What does Job, or any person, know about the mysteries of the universe? God is telling Job, and all people, that there are some things which are simply beyond our ability to understand. Only God, who created everything, can understand everything—including why people suffer.

Job understands and accepts God's answer. "I have said too much," he says. "I put my hand to my mouth."

It is a mystery why God allows people to suffer.

Why do bad things happen to good people?

This question, the same one that Job faced, comes up again and again throughout people's lives. Job struggled with this question and finally received an answer. But while suffering, many people may not find the answer given in the Book of Job all that helpful. If someone you love suddenly dies, then God's answer to Job, that people cannot understand all of God's ways, may not be enough to help you overcome your sorrow. When you are faced with personal suffering you might want to look at what Jewish thinkers have said to help other people who have been in pain.

God helps people who suffer in indirect ways

A nineteenth century Hassidic rabbi once said, "Human beings are God's language." He meant that the help and comfort people give each other in times of pain and stress are actions that come from God.

Perhaps it is God who inspires people to apply their skills and intelligence towards eliminating some of the world's problems. Maybe it is God who moves people to risk their own lives saving others when a flood devastates a town.

And God helps people who suffer by giving them the strength to continue living meaningful and productive lives. Many people find this strength by learning how to help others. A person crippled in a diving accident might dedicate himself to teaching others how to dive safely. Or he might work as a therapist with people more handicapped than he.

Suffering often teaches us lessons that help us become better people. If you have ever had to walk on crutches, for example, you will probably feel more sympathy for a person who has lost a leg and can never walk again.

Judaism teaches that only God knows why people suffer. But that does not mean that each of us should not try to find our own answers. Through the Book of Job and the teachings of the rabbis, you may find answers that will give you strength to face the difficult times in your life.

But one thing is clear. Suffering does not prove that there is no God. It only means that Jews must devote their lives to help reduce suffering and must try to know God and God's ways.

<table>
<tr><td>

CHAPTER

5

</td></tr>
</table>

Live and Let Live

The school bell rang, announcing the end of another long Friday afternoon. Dennis stuffed his books in his pack and ran outside. He weaved past groups of other ninth graders until he found his own friends. There they were, waiting for him on the sidewalk, talking about their weekend plans.

"Listen to this," Jason said as they started walking home. "I'm actually going out with Susan tomorrow night. Can you believe it?"

"No," said Greg. "She's really cute. What are you going to do?"

"We're going to the Superman movie down at the mall. Her sister said she'd drive us there and then come back around midnight to pick us up."

Brad informed the group that he had already seen the movie. "It's excellent. And besides, I saw it for free."

"How did you do that?" everyone asked at once.

"Simple. That theater's really easy to sneak into. Jason, here's what you do. Walk around the parking lot and look for the back exit on the left side . . ."

"Wait a second, Brad," Dennis broke in. "You're telling Jason to do something wrong. If he doesn't pay for the ticket, it's like he's stealing from the theater."

"Oh, give me a break," Greg said. "It's not really stealing —nobody's taking anything. Everyone does it, anyway."

"That doesn't make it right," Dennis answered. "Stealing is wrong no matter how many people do it."

"Oh, they'll never notice it. And it's their own fault, charging so much for a crummy two-hour show."

Jason spoke. "Listen, Dennis," he said to his friend, "these guys are just trying to help me save some money and look good in front of Susan. That's not so bad, is it? They're not asking you to do it. So you do what's right for you and I'll do what's right for me."

The three boys dropped back, listening as Brad revealed his theater-entering technique. Up ahead, Dennis walked alone.

• *Did Dennis have the right to tell Jason what to do and what not to do?*
• *When two people disagree on what is right and what is wrong, how do you decide whom to follow?*
• *Is every person's opinion about what is right and what is wrong equally correct?*

God is the highest authority

This story describes the problem that arises when there are two or more opinions about what is right and what is wrong, and there is no higher authority who must be obeyed. This problem is similar to one that would occur in a basketball game if there was no rule book and no referee. Imagine the chaos that would erupt if one team called a foul, the other team claimed that no foul took place, and there was no rule book or referee that both teams had to obey! So, too, in real life, when there is no highest authority that all people obey, there is no way to decide who is right and who is wrong.

Judaism's basic teaching is that God is the world's highest authority. God is higher than all people, societies, and governments. The Jews' primary task, therefore, is to ensure that all people recognize God as the highest authority and obey God's rules. Just as basketball teams must all recognize a highest authority and rule book, so must all people recognize a higher authority and rule book. God's rules, not people's opinions, determine what is right and what is wrong. Some of these rules are contained in the Torah. The most well known are the Ten Commandments. They first told the world that God forbids murder and stealing. The Torah and other Jewish sources contain many other rules about what is right and what is wrong.

God and God's laws define good and evil

Without God's laws, people have only their own opinions to rely on in determining what is good and what is bad. As a result, even an entire society, with millions of people, can say that a bad thing is good, or at least not really bad. Before the American Civil War, many white Southerners owned black men and women who had been kidnapped from Africa. The whites considered them mere property, and denied them basic human rights. Although some white Southerners considered slavery evil, most white people in the South did not regard it as morally wrong.

In the story, only Dennis said that sneaking into a movie theater was stealing. All his friends disagreed. They said it was not really wrong, even if it was a form of stealing.

People can do very bad things when they rely only on their own or other people's opinions to determine what is right and wrong and how they should act. Why?

First of all, they can call whatever they do good — no matter how bad it is. After all, if everything is a matter of opinion, then people can do the most terrible things and say that in their opinion, it is all right. Secondly, if good and evil are determined by people's opinions, then it is easy to justify doing a bad thing by saying "everyone else is doing it, so it can't be that bad." This is exactly how Greg defended stealing, and how many white Southerners came to defend kidnapping black people and making them slaves.

For these reasons, it is necessary to have moral laws from God. Without God, right and wrong are just a matter of personal opinion. Stealing from a movie theater is wrong, but not because Dennis says so. Kidnapping people to be slaves is wrong, but not because Abraham Lincoln said so. God, not people's opinions, decides what is right and what is wrong.

This is why the Jews' task of spreading ethical monotheism is so important. The world must recognize that God is the source of right and wrong, and that God demands right actions from everyone. Until this happens, every individual and every society will continue to have their own opinions about right and wrong. And they will continue to justify doing terrible things to others on the grounds that "in their opinion," what they are doing is all right.

People need God and God's laws to guide them in deciding what is right and what is wrong.

<table>
<tr><td>**CHAPTER**
6</td><td></td></tr>
</table>

Should the Majority Rule?

Judy's mother was annoyed. *"It's time you stopped sulking,"* she said to her daughter. *"We're here to stay. I've seen lots of kids your age in the neighborhood. Please go out and try to make some new friends."*

Without answering, Judy grabbed her sweatshirt and headed for the park. She recognized one of the more popular groups from school. Judy watched them enviously, wondering what it would be like to sit with them on the grass, talking and laughing. She sat down near the edge of the circle and listened.

"That ugly old witch, who does she think she is, anyway?" complained Ron, the group's leader.

"Yeah, just for walking on her precious lawn," Susie said.

"If you don't get off my lawn I'll call the police and I'm not going to warn you again!" Bruce's whining imitation of Mrs. Crankcase, the elderly and nervous widow, made everyone laugh.

"We'll get even with her," Ron said.

Suddenly Susie noticed Judy and said "I saw you in school today. You're new in this neighborhood, aren't you?"

"Yes, we just moved here from Chicago. My name's Judy."

"Why don't you walk to school with us tomorrow morning?" Ron asked.

"Sure."

"We'll pick you up at seven-thirty. Where do you live?"

Thrilled at the invitation, Judy pointed to her house across the street. The next day, as the group was walking to school, they saw Mrs. Crankcase's car pull out of her driveway.

"Now's our chance," Bruce said. "Let's go! We can walk on her lawn as much as we want."

The kids laughed and yelled as they ran up and down the lawn. Then they heard the barking of Mrs. Crankcase's German shepherd, who was tied up in the backyard.

"You stupid dog!" Ron shouted. "We'll shut you up! Everybody grab a rock and follow me!"

Judy froze in shock when Ron aimed a rock at the dog's head. Everyone in the group took a turn. Each blow brought a yelp from the helpless animal.

Ron put a rock in Judy's hand. "Go ahead," he said, "throw it."

"I can't," said Judy, after some hesitation. "It's wrong."

"But Judy, the old bag deserves it," said Susie, "and so does her stupid dog. We're all doing it, and we can't all be wrong, can we?"

"But you're hurting the dog," Judy protested.

"Don't worry, he'll be OK tomorrow. Besides, he can't tell on us. Look Judy, are you with us or not?"

Judy wanted desperately to be part of this group. Maybe Susie was right, she thought. They couldn't all be wrong. She raised her arm and threw the rock.

QUESTIONS FOR DISCUSSION
* *Why did Judy decide to throw the rock? What were her choices?*
* *Why did the kids decide to throw stones at the dog? Do you think that they had a good reason?*
* *If an entire group of people decide that something is right, does that make it right?*

God's authority is higher than a society's authority

Ron and his friends decided it was right to hurt Mrs. Crankcase's dog. They determined what was right for the whole group to follow. Judy figured that since she wanted to be part of the group, she had to obey the group's decision and hurt the dog. She did something she knew was wrong because the group said that it was right, and she wanted to be part of the group.

A society is a large group. It makes laws and requires people to obey them. But sometimes a society's laws go against the laws of God. Such a society has forgotten or denies that the highest authority belongs to God. Judaism's basic teaching is that what God says is right is more important than what any individual or society says is right.

God is the highest authority, and right and wrong are determined by God and God's laws. No matter how many people do evil—even if a whole society does evil—the evil act does not become right.

When people and societies do evil they often call it "good"

The kids in the story said they had a good reason to throw rocks at the dog. They said that they had a right to get back at Mrs. Crankcase for yelling at them.

When societies pass bad laws or commit evil acts, they also say, and they may even really believe, that they have good reasons. In the name of making a better Germany, Hitler and the Nazis murdered six million Jews and started a war that killed at least forty-nine million others. In the name of building the Soviet Union, Stalin and the Communists murdered twenty million Russians, Ukrainians and others. Other societies and many individuals who have done terrible things have called those things "good." But no matter what any person or society might say, the question remains: Is this act right or wrong according to God?

Individuals have a difficult choice when a group or society urges them to do something wrong. They can do what the group wants or they can remember that God is the highest authority and follow God's laws. Judy couldn't resist the pressures of the group. Maybe she had never learned that God's laws forbid causing unnecessary pain to animals. If she knew that she was actually choosing between God's laws and the group's laws, she might have done the right thing.

When God is not recognized as the highest authority, Greg and Brad can steal, Judy and the group can hurt the helpless dog, and tyrants like Hitler and Stalin can murder millions of innocent people.

God's authority is higher than that of people, governments and societies.

PART TWO
Why We Need Laws

Camp Sitting Duck

The Baseball League was one of Camp Sitting Duck's most popular traditions. There were two teams, the Eagles and the Braves. They met twice a week, on Monday and Thursday afternoons, for a rousing game of baseball. At the end of the summer the team with the best record was declared champion.

On the second day of camp all of the ninth grade boys assembled on the baseball field to choose sides for the first big game. David and Larry, two of the stars from the previous summer, were named captains of the teams. All of the boys waited expectantly as David and Larry picked their teammates one by one. Competition mounted through several rounds of choosing until there were only six campers left.

"I'll take Stan," Larry called out, feeling that he had chosen the best player of the remaining six boys.

"OK, we'll go with Syd," countered the Eagle's captain, David.

Syd, a short camper, ran over to his new teammates, relieved that he had not been chosen last.

Harry, another short camper, was chosen next by Larry. Steven, tall and akward, went to David's team. Larry made his last choice.

"Harvey," he called. But Harvey, the camp intellectual, was too engrossed in his physics book to hear his name. One of the Braves grabbed his elbow and led him over to the rest of the team.

"I guess that leaves Morris," said David.

Morris, the fattest boy in the camp, was always picked last. He walked slowly towards his teammates, carefully avoiding their eyes.

From the Eagles' bench, Jerry yelled "Nice going, guys! You're stuck with Morris the Blimp! Hope he doesn't weigh you down too much!"

"That's enough. Everyone to his team. Let's play ball," said Big Foot, the head counselor.

At dinner that night the boys talked of nothing but the upcoming game. Morris kept quiet. He knew that anything he said would be laughed at. He ate silently, but even that brought ridicule from his bunkmates.

"Hey Morris," Jerry said, "Why don't you go on a diet so we can find your chin?" All the guys howled with laughter, except David, who looked away, and Harvey, who was reading his book. Morris stared down at his plate.

Greg spoke next. "This little piggie went to market, this little piggie stayed home, and this little piggie went to Camp Sitting Duck!"

They laughed so loudly and for so long that the head counselor came over to their table. "What's going on here?" he asked.

"Nothing. We're just reciting our favorite nursery rhymes."

Jerry was a master at playing innocent. The other boys tried to control their laughter.

"May I be excused?" asked Morris, "I don't feel too well."

"What's the matter, Morris?" the counselor asked.

"May I please go back to my cabin?"

"OK, I'll walk you there," responded the counselor.

As soon as Morris had gone, Jerry leaned in to the center of the table. "I've got an idea," he said in a near-whisper that the counselors couldn't hear. "Let's get some frogs from the creek and put them into Morris's bed. He'll have a nice surprise when he wakes up."

"Sounds great," responded all the guys, except David, who said nothing, and Harvey, who was still reading his book.

That night, Jerry, Greg and Marshall slipped out of the cabin. They caught some frogs and brought them back to the bed where Morris was sleeping. Stan and Steve stood guard.

In the next bed, David lay awake. He did not want to participate. Harvey hid under his blankets with a flashlight, reading his book.

Two days later, Morris's parents came and took him home.

QUESTIONS FOR DISCUSSION
- Was Jerry's behavior good or bad? How about the way his friends, Greg and Marshall, acted?
- What about Stan and Steve? David? Harvey?
- Why did most of the boys hurt Morris rather than try to help him?
- Could the counselor have done anything to prevent the boys' cruelty to Morris? If you were the counselor, what would you have done?

Every person has the capacity to do good or to do bad

Judaism recognizes the existence of both good and bad forces within every human being. These forces are not mysterious or unknown. In fact, everyone experiences them every day in choosing to do right or wrong.

In Hebrew these forces are called the **yetzer ha-tov** and the **yetzer ha-ra**. *Yetzer* means a creative force, *tov* means good, and *ra* means bad. *Yetzer ha-tov*, therefore, means the "creative force for doing good," and *yetzer ha-ra* means the "creative force for doing bad." Since these forces are present in every person, all people have the capacity to do good or to do bad.

The struggle between the yetzer ha-tov and the yetzer ha-ra

When people have to choose between good and bad they are faced with an inner struggle. While the *yetzer ha-tov* pushes them to do what is right, the *yetzer ha-ra* pulls them in the opposite direction.

Here are two examples of how the *yetzer ha-tov* and the *yetzer ha-ra* can operate.

Case 1: You are at the check-out counter at the supermarket. You have just bought some of your favorite chocolate. The clerk makes a mistake and gives you more change than you deserve. Your first thought is:

"What luck. I got all this chocolate for free."

A split second later, however, you find yourself thinking:

"It's not my money. The right thing to do would be to tell the clerk about the error and return the money."

The first thought, to keep the money, is a greedy one. It might be called the "pull" of the *yetzer ha-ra*. The second thought, to return the money, is an honest one. It shows the "pull" of the *yetzer ha-tov*.

Case 2: It is 3:30 P.M. You run through the school building eager to leave to meet your friends for ice cream. But as you pass Susan's locker, she stops you.

"Can you help me catch up with all the assignments I missed when I was sick?"

You know that helping Susan will take at least half an hour. Your first thought is:

"I'd rather be with my friends. I'll tell Susan that I have to go to the dentist."

A split second later, you say to yourself:

"I should help her. She's got so much catching up to do. My friends will wait for me if I'm late."

The first thought, a selfish one, shows the pull of the *yetzer ha-ra*. The second thought shows kindness and the pull of the *yetzer ha-tov*.

"The heart of man leans towards his yetzer ha-ra from his youth"

Everyone experiences similar struggles between his or her *yetzer ha-tov* and *yetzer ha-ra*. Judaism also teaches that it is usually easier to follow the *yetzer ha-ra* than to follow the *yetzer ha-tov*.

Why did most of the boys in the story participate in hurting Morris? Their treatment of Morris was very cruel. And yet, it is not an unusual form of behavior among teenagers. Take an honest look at yourself and your friends. How would you treat an unpopular kid like Morris, or anyone else who did not fit in with your group?

Chances are that at some time or other, you have behaved like Jerry and Greg behaved towards Morris. The fact that you may have acted cruelly does not mean that you are always a cruel person. It does mean that at times you have followed your *yetzer ha-ra*. People often give in to their bad instincts. The Torah says, "The heart of man leans towards his *yetzer ha-ra* from his youth." It is usually much easier to do bad, or to do nothing, than it is to do good.

It's harder to do good than to do bad

Think of things that are hard to do, like playing chess or a musical instrument. You must put in many hours of study and practice to do them well. In the same way, people have to work at being good. They need to learn rules for good behavior, and they need to discipline themselves to follow those rules. This discipline does not come naturally; it requires a lot of time, effort, and energy. It is difficult to go out of your way to help people, and to make sure that you are always trying to do the right thing. It is much easier not to put forth this effort but rather continue leaning towards the *yetzer ha-ra*.

Another reason it is harder to do good than to do bad is that doing good often means going against the crowd. In the story, it was Jerry's suggestion to put the frogs into Morris's bed, but almost all of the boys went along with it. They did not have the strength and courage needed to fight for what is right against a group of people; they followed the easier path of going along with the crowd or doing nothing.

Because doing good requires constant effort and the strength and courage to stand up for what is right, it is easier to lean towards the *yetzer ha-ra* than the *yetzer ha-tov*.

People must make a strong and constant effort to be good.

What is a good person?

Many people think that they are good as long as they don't hurt anybody. This is wrong. Suppose someone in your school has broken a leg. You see him walking down the hall, struggling with his crutches and his books. If you walk by without offering to help, are you a good person? You might say yes, because you have done nothing to hurt him.

But Jewish law says no. According to Judaism, a person who merely doesn't hurt others is not a good person. This person is simply not a criminal. Judaism teaches that a good person is someone who actively does good deeds.

In the above situation, to be a good person you would have to take an active step to help the person with the broken leg. For instance, you could carry his books for him to his next class. Or you could walk next to him, lending him a supporting arm. These acts, as opposed to doing nothing at all, would fit the Jewish definition of a good person.

According to Judaism, a good person is one who actively does good.

"Do not stand by while your neighbor's blood is being shed"

By Jewish standards, the behavior of Jerry, Greg, Marshall, Stan and Steve was clearly wrong. They planned and carried out actions to hurt Morris.

Although it may not be as easy to see, David and Harvey were also in the wrong and were not following some important Jewish laws. David did not like what the boys were doing to Morris, and he did not join them. But he did nothing to stop them, either. By not doing anything, he was contributing to Morris's suffering. Even though it would have been difficult, he should have had the courage to defend Morris. If his bunkmates then ignored his complaint, he should have gone to the counselor for help.

Jewish law states, "Do not stand by while your neighbor's blood is being shed." You are not permitted to stand by and do nothing as someone is being hurt. David saw Morris, his neighbor at the dinner table, get hurt. But he stood by and did nothing. According to Jewish law, while David did not act as badly as the others, neither did he act like a good person.

A good person makes every possible effort to prevent evil. In fact, because David could have made the situation better, but did not, he was also responsible for Morris's leaving camp.

"Get rid of the evil around you"

Harvey was deeply absorbed in his book. He may not have realized what was happening around him. Despite this fact, he, too, was not good and was responsible for Morris's leaving camp. According to Jewish law, you must get rid of the evil that is around you. By not being aware of what was happening to Morris, Harvey was allowing evil to continue.

Harvey should have been aware of his bunkmates nasty pranks and he should have done something to stop them. It is true that Harvey was occupied with other activities, but Judaism teaches that this does not free a person from the responsibility to "get rid of evil."

Jews are required to fight evil, even though it often happens to people they do not know and even when they do not actually see the evil taking place. The laws, "Do not stand by while your neighbor's blood is being shed" and "You must get rid of the evil that is around you," require you to fight evil and try to improve the world. It is not enough to "not hurt others" in a world where so many people are suffering, like the poor in your own community, or Jews in the Soviet Union.

You must be aware of evil in order to fight it.

People need to be taught to be good

People have both a *yetzer ha-tov* and a *yetzer ha-ra*. But it is easier to follow the *yetzer ha-ra* than the *yetzer ha-tov* because goodness requires effort, discipline, strength and courage. And further, to be a good person, you must actively do good. For these reasons, it is very important to teach people to be good. If the counselor and the parents of the kids in the story had understood this, they would have taught these kids about sensitivity to other people's feelings. And they would have given them some basic rules to follow. They should have warned them that they would be punished if they acted cruelly. If they had done these things, there is a good chance that Morris would not have been treated so badly by his bunkmates.

It is not easy to be a good person. It is not easy to find the courage needed to go against a crowd, or the discipline needed to take active steps against evil. Just like the kids at Camp Sitting Duck, people need rules on how to be good.

CHAPTER 8

Lost City of Atlantis

Hey Clark!" yelled Lois Trent from the other side of the room. "The chief wants to see you. I think he wants to give you a new assignment."

"OK, Lois, thanks." Timidly, Clark approached his editor's desk. "You wanted to see me, boss?"

"Clark, I want you to get on this immediately! Remember the story you wrote about that new ideal city, Atlantis, and how it was formed?"

"Yeah, sure, boss. I remember it. That's the place where they believe that people are naturally good. So they have no laws, and the citizens are allowed to do whatever they feel is right."

"That's the place, all right. Well, there are rumors that things aren't so hot down there. I want you to find out what's going on in Atlantis and why they have so many problems."

"Sure, boss, sure," Clark said. "Right away. Consider the job done." Clark nearly tripped over his own feet as he left the editor's office. He was nervous about this new assignment.

"Oh, golly! Gee whiz. How am I ever going to get to the bottom of this story? Let's see . . . what can I do? I've got it! I'll drop in on the mayor of Atlantis and ask him. In fact, I'll just fill up the car and leave tonight."

Atlantis was a long night's drive away. An exhausted Clark entered the gates of the city about two hours after dawn.

The highway was crowded, and cars were not traveling in any particular lane. They were, in fact, weaving around each other at very high speeds.

"Wow! Seems to be rush hour," Clark said to himself. At that moment, a car zoomed by, missing him by a fraction of an inch. "Whew! That was a close one. These cars are moving awfully fast. I wonder what the speed limit is here." Then he saw the sign: Speed Limit: Whatever Speed You Feel Is Right.

And if that sign didn't make him nervous enough, Clark then noticed all the wrecked, abandoned vehicles scattered along both sides of the road. Realizing it would be safer to get exact directions to the mayor's office so he could continue his investigation, Clark carefully pulled over to the side of the road and parked his car. Clark then spotted three teenagers playing ball in a nearby lot. He approached them, held out the address he had written down, and asked, "Hey, kids! Can you tell me how to get to this address?"

"Sorry, mister. None of us can read. Where do you want to go?"

"You can't read?! Why not?" asked Clark in astonishment. "And by the way, what are you doing out of school in the middle of the morning?"

"In Atlantis, we only have to go to school if we feel like it. And to tell you the truth, we'd rather play ball."

After getting directions to the mayor's office, Clark got back into his car. He carefully drove the few short blocks to City Hall. Glancing out the car window Clark noticed that the streets were littered with trash. People didn't use the trash cans that were provided for litter. They simply dropped their wrappers on the ground.

Clark finally arrived in front of City Hall. He saw the parking lot but could not enter it. There were available spaces in the lot but all four driveways were blocked by cars parked across them. There were even a few cars parked on the sidewalk.

Frustrated, Clark circled the block. Suddenly he realized that he didn't need to see the mayor after all. He already knew why the city of Atlantis was in so much trouble. He drove home to write his story.

QUESTIONS FOR DISCUSSION
- *What was the problem in Atlantis?*
- *Why didn't the speed limit sign work in controlling the traffic?*
- *Can a society function when it is guided only by what each person feels is right?*

Why Atlantis didn't work

The founders of Atlantis believed that people are basically good and therefore do not need laws to tell them how to act. Each citizen of Atlantis was allowed to decide for himself what was right. What was the result of this philosophy?

People need laws and restrictions to ensure that they do good. Otherwise, people will usually do only what is good for themselves. This is why on the highways of Atlantis, most people drove without concern for anyone else's safety; and why in their neighborhoods, they dropped trash on the streets and sidewalks. The people of Atlantis, like people anywhere, were more interested in their own needs and desires than in the needs and desires of others. Atlantis's system did not work because it expected people to be good without giving them guidelines for goodness.

The need for studying and practicing goodness

Judaism is based on the idea that people need laws in order to do good. That is why Judaism is a religion of laws. To master any skill or subject, from carpentry to medicine to literature, people must study and follow rules. In the same way, goodness is a skill that must be studied. It, too, has rules that must be followed. Unfortunately, however, while almost all students must study physics, English, art, and literature, almost no students are required to study goodness.

Everyone has the capacity to be good in the same way that everyone has the capacity to play the piano. To become a good pianist, a person must study music and practice diligently for years. Similarly, an individual must study the meaning of goodness and practice doing good deeds to become a good person.

Being good depends on how you act, not how you feel

Judaism teaches that a good person is someone who does good deeds. Some examples of these deeds which are listed in the Torah and the Talmud are: visiting the sick; giving charity; and making sure that your animal is fed before you feed yourself. According to Jewish law, goodness is based on actions, not feelings; therefore, how you act is more important than how you feel.

Since it is Judaism's goal that people do good, actions are what matter most. While good feelings are wonderful, they do not nec-

essarily lead to good actions. Imagine that your aunt is ill and is hospitalized. While you might feel upset and very sorry for her, these feelings will not necessarily cause you to visit her. You might feel like you should visit her, but if it is inconvenient, you might find reasons why you just can't make it.

What would really be good for your aunt is for you to spend some time with her. Just thinking about visiting does not help your aunt at all. Unless you actually visit your sick aunt, you are not doing good in this particular situation. Having good intentions is helpful, but if they do not cause you to do something good, those intentions and feelings are of little importance. Good intentions are often not enough to produce good actions.

The deed shapes the heart

Judaism teaches that good actions are more likely to lead to good intentions than good intentions are to lead to good actions.

Imagine that you do go to visit your sick aunt. You may not be very enthusiastic about it because you have plenty of other things to do that afternoon. But you go because you know that it is the right thing to do. By the end of the visit, both you and your aunt will feel better. She will feel better because your visit has brought her a little comfort and companionship; you will feel better because you have done something good for someone else.

Can you remember any time this happened to you in the past? Was there a situation where you helped someone, even though you did not start out really wanting to do so? Perhaps you visited a hospital with your class or you helped someone who was in trouble. How did you feel once the deed was completed? It is very likely that you found yourself feeling good about what you had done. And you probably felt better about yourself as a person because you did good. When you do something good and see the results, it is very likely that you will want to do, and will do, more good acts more often.

The idea that good actions lead you to develop good intentions can be stated as "the deed shapes the heart." In other words, the more good deeds you do, the more you will want to do good in the future.

Judaism teaches that your actions are more important than your intentions.

Laws are necessary to make good people and a good society

People need guidelines to act good. In a family, parents usually make rules like "call your grandmother once a week" or "do not interrupt when someone is speaking." Societies have laws and regulations such as "do not litter" or "those returning library books late will be fined." These laws, rules, and regulations all have the same purpose: to have people do good and to make a good society. Thus, the purpose of a speed limit is to save lives on the highway. And the law against littering keeps parks and streets clean for everyone's enjoyment.

The city of Atlantis had no laws or regulations. People did whatever they wanted to do. Instead of the ideal society its founders intended, Atlantis became a city filled with terrible problems and disorder. Guidelines are needed to create good people and laws are needed to create a good and orderly society.

Laws are not enough

Atlantis was a bad society because it had no laws. However, some societies might have laws and still be bad. There are two possible reasons for this. First, the laws can be bad laws, and second, even if the laws are good ones, they are worthless if they are not enforced.

The Soviet Union provides both examples. First, it has some evil laws. One such law is that the border police must shoot any Soviet citizen who tries to cross into another country. Second, the Soviet Union also has some good laws. One such law prohibits anti-Semitism and another one guarantees freedom of speech. But these laws are worthless because they are never enforced; in fact, they are ignored. The United States also has good laws, but unlike the Soviet Union, it tries to enforce them. A society like the United States, which has good laws and enforces them, is a good society.

If the goal of a society is to create a good world and good people, a system of good laws is needed. While there are numerous systems of laws, there is one which has worked in creating a good people for about 3,000 years. This is the system of the *mitzvot* in Judaism.

People need laws to become good people, to create good societies, and to make the world a better place.

CHAPTER 9

The Quickest Way to Torah

*O*nce there was a young non-Jew who wanted to learn about Judaism. His name was Zane and he liked to ask clever and challenging questions. Zane decided to track down two of the greatest rabbis of the time and to present each of them with a difficult challenge. One of the rabbis was called Shammai, and the other was called Hillel. Zane entered the house of Shammai first.

"Rabbi! I challenge you! If you can teach me the entire Torah while I stand on one foot, I'll become a Jew."

Shammai could not believe his ears. What arrogance this man had, asking to learn the whole Torah within a few minutes! The rabbi refused to answer, and sent him on his way.

The next day the man entered the house of Hillel, the other great rabbi, and issued the same challenge:

"Rabbi! Teach me the entire Torah while standing on one foot. If you can do that, I will convert to Judaism."

Hillel realized that he was being challenged. But rather than become angry, he showed patience and wisdom. He wanted to give the young man the best answer that he could.

"Are you ready? Are you standing on one foot?" Hillel said.

"Yes, rabbi, go ahead," answered Zane, amazed that the rabbi was responding to his challenge.

"Do not do to others what you would not like done to yourself. All the rest of the Torah is an explanation of this rule. Now, my boy, go and study."

QUESTIONS FOR DISCUSSION
• *Repeat Hillel's famous teaching in your own words. What does it mean to you?*
• *Give five examples of how you can put Hillel's guideline into practice.*

Judaism is a system of laws

One of Judaism's main goals is to make good people and a better world. To do that, Judaism provides guidelines, or laws, for Jews to follow. The laws cover every phase of life: from childhood to adulthood; at home, at school, and at work. The laws tell Jews how to conduct themselves at all times.

Some Jewish laws have existed for over 3,000 years. Some of them, such as the laws concerned with the ancient Temple, are not applicable today. But most Jewish laws are as applicable today as they were in ancient times.

Before you can begin to study specific Jewish laws and their meanings, however, you must understand some basic definitions and learn about the Jewish texts in which the laws are found. Then you will be prepared to study and understand Jewish law, which is the basis of Judaism.

Mitzvah does not mean good deed

Mitzvah is often used to mean good deed. While a good deed is a *mitzvah*, that is not what the word means. *Mitzvah* means commandment. The difference is important. A good deed is something you might choose to do. A commandment is something you are obligated to do.

The plural of *mitzvah* is *mitzvot*. The *mitzvot*, or commandments, are Judaism's laws for making good people and a better world. The *mitzvot* are found in two main sources: the Bible and the Talmud.

The Bible

Three separate sections make up the Bible: **Torah, Nevi'im** and **K'tuvim**. Take the first Hebrew letters of each word, *taff, nun,* and *kaf,* and you get the Hebrew word for the Bible, **Tanach**.

The first section, the Torah, is composed of the five books of Moses: Genesis; Exodus; Leviticus; Numbers; and Deuteronomy. Every Shabbat, a **parasha** (portion) of these five books is read in synagogue.

The second section of the Tanach is the Nevi'im, which means Prophets. It contains the history and the messages of the prophets. Every Shabbat, a portion of the Nevi'im is read; that portion is called the **Haftarah**.

The K'tuvim, the Writings, is the third section of the Tanach and contains books dealing with Jewish history and Jewish thought. For example, the **Megillat Esther**, read on Purim, is found in the K'tuvim. Perhaps the most inspiring book in the K'tuvim is **Tehillim**, Psalms, which contain poems about the relationship between God and the Jew.

The Tanach, a main source of mitzvot, has three sections: Torah, Nevi'im, and K'tuvim.

The Torah contains 613 mitzvot

Some of the most basic laws of our civilization come directly from the Torah. Consider such laws as "Do not murder" or "Love your neighbor as yourself." Not just Jews, but most people everywhere, accept these laws as the foundation of a just and compassionate society.

Judaism teaches that the Torah contains 613 *mitzvot*. Besides the *mitzvot*, the Torah also offers stories that teach people about God, and about the difference between right and wrong. The main purpose of these stories is to teach you how to lead your life.

The Talmud: a second source of mitzvot

Approximately 1,500 years after the Torah was received, the **Talmud** was written. The Talmud has many volumes and is composed of two sections, the **Mishnah** and the **Gemarah**. The Mishnah contains laws that are additions to and explanations of the laws found in the Torah. The Gemarah contains explanations and additions to the laws of the Mishnah. The Talmud recorded the important discussions about the laws which took place between the major rabbis, teachers and scholars of the period between 200 B.C.E. and 500 C.E. The rabbis spent long hours debating and interpreting the *mitzvot* so they could be applied to everyday life. In fact, the story about the man asking Hillel and Shammai to explain Judaism while standing on one leg is found in the Gemarah.

In addition to the Tanach, the Talmud is the other great source of Jewish law.

Some examples of mitzvot found in the Talmud

The *mitzvot* found in the Talmud are usually based on the *mitzvot* found in the Torah. As the rabbis of that period discussed and interpreted the Torah they recorded additional *mitzvot* for Jews to follow. Take the *mitzvah* from the Torah "Love your neighbor as yourself," as an example. To this original commandment, the Talmud adds the following *mitzvot*.

1. *Let the honor of your fellow man be as precious to you as your own.* This *mitzvah* is concerned with protecting the honor and reputation of other people. It means that you should respect another person's dignity and feelings as you would your own. If someone in your class makes a mistake while answering a question, you should not laugh or ridicule him. Imagine your own feelings if other people laughed at you, and let that thought guide your action.

2. *Let the property of your fellow man be as precious to you as your own.* This *mitzvah* is concerned with respecting things that belong to other people. If you borrow a record from a friend, you should be as careful not to damage it as you would be with a record of your own.

The Talmud explained, interpreted, and added more *mitzvot* to the *mitzvot* of the Torah. Together, the Torah and the Talmud contain most of Judaism's *mitzvot*, and they are the foundation of the Jewish legal system. This system provides everyday guidelines for making better people and for building a better world.

The two main sources of the *mitzvot* are the Torah and the Talmud.

PART THREE

Mitzvot Between People

CHAPTER 10

Treasure Hunt

*A*s long as she could remember, Samantha had wanted her own antique store. Now, after years of scraping and saving, she had finally put together enough money to realize her dream. She found a small empty shop on Main Street and began moving in her merchandise. Finally, one sunny April morning, Samantha's Antique Shop opened its doors.

It was one of the first warm spring days of the year. By noontime the streets were filled with office workers on their lunch hour. In the park, Mr. Shapiro finished his sandwich and glanced at his watch. He still had a few minutes before he had to return to the office. He decided to visit the new antique shop he had passed on his way to work that morning.

Samantha's face brightened when she saw her first potential customer enter the store.

"Can I help you, sir?" she asked Mr. Shapiro.

"No thanks. I'm just looking. Is that all right with you?"

"Oh, of course. Please look around all you want," she said, disappointed, yet relieved to know the truth.

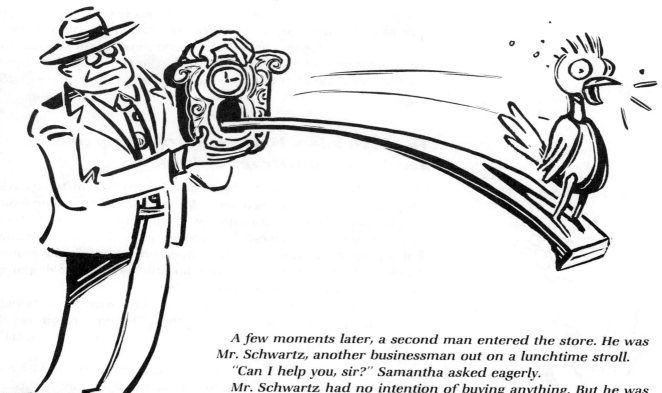

A few moments later, a second man entered the store. He was Mr. Schwartz, another businessman out on a lunchtime stroll.

"Can I help you, sir?" Samantha asked eagerly.

Mr. Schwartz had no intention of buying anything. But he was curious about the prices of the antiques.

"How much is this clock?" he asked.

"You have a good eye, sir," Samantha answered. "It's really a fine old piece of work, and worth much more than the forty-five dollars I'm asking for it. This is my first day and I'm lowering prices to get business rolling." She went on to describe the clock, which she had driven one hundred miles to buy.

"Hmm . . ." said Mr. Schwartz. "Yes, that's interesting. Well, how much is that rocking chair?"

Once again Samantha launched into an enthusiastic description. But neither her enthusiasm nor her expertise helped her sell the chair, because Mr. Schwartz had never considered buying it. After asking for a few more prices, he left the store.

Alone with her antiques, Samantha almost cried. She wondered what she had done wrong. Maybe Mr. Schwartz had disliked her. Or maybe he knew more about antiques than she did, and did not approve of her taste. And if many people agreed with him, her business might never get off the ground!

QUESTIONS FOR DISCUSSION
• Why was Samantha so upset?
• Who showed more sensitivity to Samantha, Mr. Shapiro or Mr. Schwartz? Why?
• Did Mr. Schwartz break any laws?

Two categories of Jewish law

The main purpose of Jewish law is to produce good people and a better world. By properly observing Jewish laws, a Jew does good and becomes a better person.

The laws, or *mitzvot*, can be divided into two categories. The *mitzvot* called **beyn adam l'havero** are concerned with relationships between people. The *mitzvot* called **beyn adam la-Makom** are concerned with people's relationship to God. Together these *mitzvot* aim to develop people who are good on the inside as well as good on the outside.

The beyn adam l'havero mitzvot help people develop sensitivity towards others

In the story, Mr. Shapiro clearly showed more sensitivity towards Samantha than did Mr. Schwartz. Mr. Shapiro did not know Samantha personally. He was not aware of how much work, time and money she had invested in the store. Yet because he knew that it is wrong to raise anyone's hopes unnecessarily, he immediately told Samantha that he was not interested in buying anything. Mr. Shapiro acted with sensitivity.

Mr. Schwartz, however, acted without sensitivity. Even though he had no intention of buying anything, he continued to ask prices. He thought only of his own curiosity, not of Samantha's feelings.

Mr. Schwartz did not break any of the country's laws, but he did break a Jewish law. In the Talmud it says: A Jew may not ask a storekeeper the price of an item which he knows he will not buy.

This *mitzvah* about not asking prices falls into the category of the *beyn adam l'havero mitzvot* which instruct the Jew how to act toward others. Judaism is so concerned with how people treat each other, and their sensitivity to others' feelings, that it even has a law about what Jews are permitted to say to a storekeeper. Thus, a Jew is not permitted to raise a storekeeper's hopes by asking the prices of items when, in fact, he has no intention of buying any of them. While Jews are, of course, permitted to compare prices while shopping, they are commanded to consider their own intentions before asking about prices.

This specific *mitzvah* does not deal with a "life or death" matter, just as most things in life do not, either. Life consists of hundreds and thousands of small actions, and it is these, as well as "life and death" matters, that are important in Judaism.

The goal of laws such as the "storekeeper law," is that Jews learn that every individual is important and deserves to be treated with kindness and sensitivity. These *mitzvot* remind Jews that all individuals—whether a shopkeeper, a bus driver, a doctor or a teacher—are far more than what they do for a living. They are human beings with a life outside of the specific role in which they are seen by others.

Hillel taught, "Do not treat others as you would not want to be treated yourself."

If Mr. Schwartz had obeyed this rule, he would have seen Samantha not just as a storekeeper, but also as a fellow human being with her own problems, pressures, ambitions and dreams. He would have thought about how he might have felt in her situation, and shown her more consideration. If you follow Hillel's rule carefully, you will begin to see a storekeeper, a bus driver, a teacher, and everyone else, as a person just like you. The "store-keeper law" is only one of Judaism's hundreds of laws to put Hillel's rule into practice.

Treating others as you would like to be treated yourself leads to having greater sensitivity towards others.

Some other examples of beyn adam l'havero mitzvot

All of the *beyn adam l'havero mitzvot* are concerned with how people treat each other. In addition to the law about asking prices in a store, the Torah and the Talmud contain hundreds of laws dealing with interactions between people. "Do not murder," for example, is one of the basic *beyn adam l'havero mitzvot*. Another *mitzvah* in this category is "Do not steal." Another, "Do not gossip," commands Jews to protect the dignity and reputation of others.

One more example is the *mitzvah*, "Give ten percent of your income to those in need." Throughout their history, Jews have observed this law so consistently that even in the poorest Jewish communities, no Jew ever went starving.

All the *mitzvot* in the *beyn adam l'havero* category guide Jews to be just and kind, to fight evil, and to work to reduce suffering.

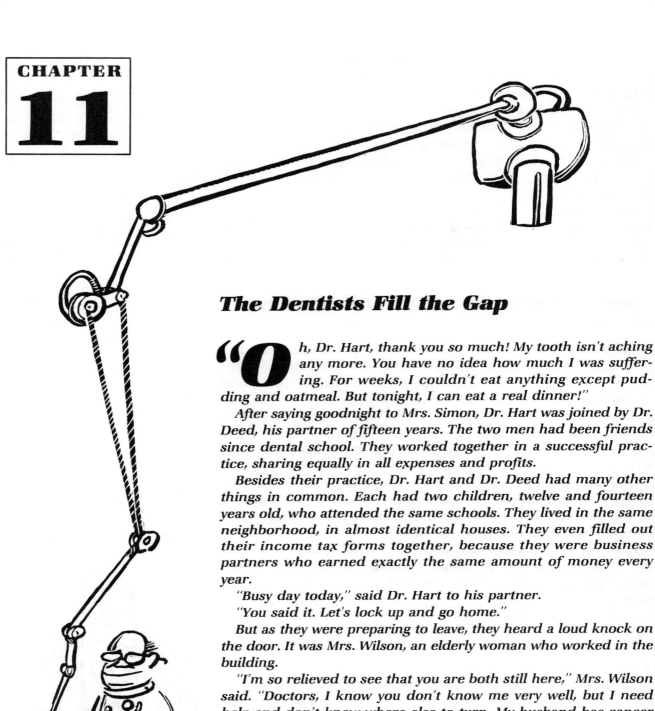

The Dentists Fill the Gap

"**O**h, Dr. Hart, thank you so much! My tooth isn't aching any more. You have no idea how much I was suffering. For weeks, I couldn't eat anything except pudding and oatmeal. But tonight, I can eat a real dinner!"

After saying goodnight to Mrs. Simon, Dr. Hart was joined by Dr. Deed, his partner of fifteen years. The two men had been friends since dental school. They worked together in a successful practice, sharing equally in all expenses and profits.

Besides their practice, Dr. Hart and Dr. Deed had many other things in common. Each had two children, twelve and fourteen years old, who attended the same schools. They lived in the same neighborhood, in almost identical houses. They even filled out their income tax forms together, because they were business partners who earned exactly the same amount of money every year.

"Busy day today," said Dr. Hart to his partner.

"You said it. Let's lock up and go home."

But as they were preparing to leave, they heard a loud knock on the door. It was Mrs. Wilson, an elderly woman who worked in the building.

"I'm so relieved to see that you are both still here," Mrs. Wilson said. "Doctors, I know you don't know me very well, but I need help and don't know where else to turn. My husband has cancer and desperately needs an operation.

"I don't have enough money, so I'm approaching not only my friends and relatives, but all the people who work in this building, too. You see, three years ago, we discovered that my husband, George, had developed stomach cancer. Since then, George has needed several operations. We've used up every source available to us, including our insurance money, and every last penny of our savings of the last thirty-five years. Unfortunately, George's medication has affected his ability to walk, and now the doctors have discovered a new tumor that must be operated on immediately."

Mrs. Wilson began to cry. "Please help us with as much money as you can."

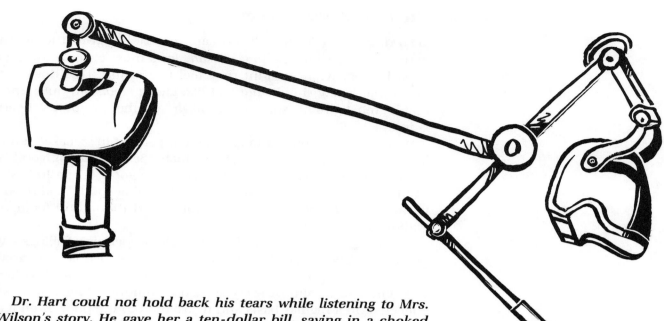

Dr. Hart could not hold back his tears while listening to Mrs. Wilson's story. He gave her a ten-dollar bill, saying in a choked voice, "I truly feel terrible for you and your husband."

During the woman's plea, Dr. Deed did not cry at all, and secretly kept looking at his watch, fearing he might be late for an appointment. But because Jewish law obligates Jews to give a certain percentage of their yearly income to people in need, and Dr. Deed tries to live by Jewish law, he wrote out a check for $250 and placed it in Mrs. Wilson's hand.

She thanked both men and went on her way.

QUESTIONS FOR DISCUSSION
- *Who did a better thing, Dr. Hart or Dr. Deed?*
- *Who helped Mrs. Wilson more?*
- *Which is more important, how you feel or how you act?*

Tzedakah does not mean charity

Both the English word charity and the Hebrew word **tzedakah** refer to helping people in need. However, there is an important difference between them. Individuals who give charity decide for themselves how much they will give. With *tzedakah*, however, individuals do not decide how much they will give—Jewish law obligates them to give a minimum amount. How much charity is given depends on the giver's feelings; how much *tzedakah* is given is based on Jewish law.

The word *tzedakah* comes from the word *tzedek*, which means justice. To give *tzedakah* is, therefore, an act of justice. And not to give *tzedakah* is an injustice.

Since doing justice is one of Judaism's basic demands, Jews have always considered *tzedakah*—taking care of the poor and less fortunate—one of Judaism's most important laws.

There are many *mitzvot* of *tzedakah*. The basic one is found in the Torah.

The law of ten percent

According to the Torah, all Jews are required to give at least ten percent of their income to *tzedakah*. Jews must observe this law regardless of what amount they feel like giving. This does not mean that a Jew should not feel like giving *tzedakah*, but rather that he must give his share of *tzedakah*, whether or not his "heart is in it."

Why are Jews required to give the ten percent to *tzedakah*, even if they do not feel like giving that much? Because doing good is more important than just feeling like doing good. While Judaism wants the Jew to do good and to feel like doing good, good deeds without good feelings do a lot more good than good feelings without good deeds.

For this reason, Judaism does not rely on people's feelings—it gives Jews laws to live by. To ensure that poor people are cared for, Judaism enacted the law of ten percent. Historically, this law was enforced in almost every Jewish community. *Tzedakah* was collected on a regular basis and distributed to the poor. Even if a Jew did not feel like giving his share, he did so because it was the Jewish law.

Today, Jews do not live in all-Jewish communities and the law of ten percent is impossible to enforce. Of course, this does not mean that Jews do not have to give their share of *tzedakah*. Each Jew must give his share, even without a request from the community.

Once a Jew becomes a bar-mitzvah, he is obligated to observe Jewish laws. And even before bar-mitzvah, it is good to begin observing *mitzvot*. *Tzedakah* does not only apply to adults or to people making a lot of money. If you receive an allowance, for example, Jewish law obligates you to give ten percent of it to *tzedakah*. And if you would rather use that money on more records, clothes or movies, then you can understand the need for the law of ten percent. You feel like spending that money on yourself, but Judaism is telling you that your feelings are less important than your helping other people.

All Jews are obligated to give ten percent of their income to *tzedakah*.

Tzedakah in action

In everyday life, situations arise which may complicate the basic law of ten percent. Over the years, the rabbis devised rules to resolve these complications. These rules can be found in many Jewish texts. One complication involved the question: Do the poor have to give *tzedakah*? Here are some examples of how *tzedakah* is applied in such special situations.

Case 1: Mr. Cohen is a retired widower who lives on a small fixed income. Although he has everything he needs, he is considered poor by the standards of his community. Is he obligated to give *tzedakah*?

Yes, he is required to give *tzedakah*, but not necessarily ten percent. According to Jewish law, even a poor man is required to give *tzedakah*, though the amount depends on what he can afford.

Case 2: Mrs. Silvers is divorced and supports her three children. Because her paycheck is never enough to cover her expenses, she receives a monthly check from Jewish Family Services. Is she obligated to give *tzedakah*?

Yes. According to Jewish law, a person who receives *tzedakah* is obligated to give some *tzedakah*, even it is only a very small amount. According to the **Shulḥan Arukh**, one of the major listings of all Jewish law, the small amount that a poor person gives is considered as worthy as the large amount given by a rich man.

Case 3: Even though Mark Greenfield was born crippled and is only nineteen years old, he manages to support himself by working in a factory. Due to his handicap, Mark is able to work only a few hours each day. If he were to give even a small amount of *tzedakah*, he would no longer be self-supporting and would soon need *tzedakah* himself. Is Mark obligated to give *tzedakah*?

No. It is against Jewish law to put yourself into the position of needing *tzedakah*.

If someone has already given his ten percent and is approached by a beggar, what should he do? "It is forbidden to turn back a poor man empty handed," says the *Shulḥan Arukh*, "even if one gives as little as a dried fig." One must always give something when approached by a person in need. "If one has nothing at all to give," continues the *Shulḥan Arukh*, "one should cheer him with words."

Maimonides and his eight degrees of tzedakah

Moses Maimonides, also known as Rambam, lived in the twelfth century. He was a rabbinic authority, a respected physician, and a brilliant Jewish philosopher. Among his many books is the **Mishneh Torah**, the most important code of Jewish law since the Talmud. In the *Mishneh Torah*, Maimonides presented a complete analysis of *tzedakah*. This analysis is still studied and observed by Jews today.

The *Mishneh Torah* lists eight different ways in which a person can give *tzedakah*. Since Maimonides believed that some ways of giving are better than others, he ranked them by numbers, or degrees. The first is the most preferred form of giving; the eighth is the least preferred.

1. Offering a man a gift or a loan, entering into partnership with him, or providing work for him so he can be self-supporting.

2. The giver and the receiver do not know each other.

3. The giver knows the receiver, but the receiver does not know the giver.

4. The giver does not know the receiver, but the receiver knows the giver.

5. The giver puts coins in the hands of the poor, without being asked.

6. The giver puts coins in the hands of the poor after being asked.

7. The giver contributes less than he should, but does so cheerfully.

8. The giver contributes with resentment, humiliating the receiver.

As you can see, Maimonides believed that it was better to give voluntarily than after being asked, and better to give cheerfully than with resentment. The important thing to note, however, is that giving, no matter how it is done, is the first step in fulfilling the *mitzvah* of *tzedakah*.

Who did a better thing, Dr. Deed or Dr. Hart?

In the story at the beginning of the chapter, more good was done by Dr. Deed than by Dr. Hart. Mrs. Wilson was helped far more by Dr. Deed's $250 than by Dr. Hart's $10 and sorrowful tears. What she most needed from the doctors was money for her husband's operation, not their sympathy. While Judaism teaches that giving cheerfully is important and desirable, the act of giving and the amount given are the essential parts of *tzedakah*.

According to Judaism, good acts are more important than good feelings. The needy are helped far more by *tzedakah* than by tears and feelings alone.

As Maimonides pointed out in his eight degrees of *tzedakah*, it is preferable that people feel good about giving. However, if the poor and needy were to wait for people to feel good before giving ten percent of their money to *tzedakah*, they would be waiting a very long time.

Jewish law commands Jews to contribute ten percent of their income towards helping the poor. It is hoped that by giving ten percent, the giver will, in time, begin to feel more like giving.

CHAPTER 12

The Tailor's Tales

Yonkel the tailor loved to gossip. That was how he survived the cold gray afternoons of winter. He would sit by the stove in his little shop, chatting with the customers. And no matter what he was doing, whether sewing at his foot-powered machine or fitting young brides in their white wedding gowns, Yonkel always managed to keep his ears open and his mouth going.

One day he heard a particularly juicy story about the town's rabbi. Mrs. Rabinowitz said she had seen the rabbi take two apples from one of the fruit stalls at the market, without leaving any money.

"But you know how our rabbi is," Mrs. Rabinowitz said to Yonkel. "So forgetful. His head was probably so full of this week's Torah portion that he must have just wandered away from the market, forgetting to pay for the fruit."

"Yes, I'm sure that's how it happened," Yonkel said.

But secretly he was delighted with this piece of news. Although he did not dislike the rabbi, he absolutely loved to gossip. So, a few minutes later, when Mr. Stitsky entered the shop, Yonkel had exciting news to tell him.

"Boy, do I have something interesting to tell you," Yonkel burst out. "The rabbi is a real phony. He tells us not to steal, but he himself goes around stealing! Just yesterday he took two big red apples from the market without paying for them. You know, I've always wondered how he can afford those fine dresses for his wife on his tiny synagogue salary."

Mr. Stitsky paid for his new coat and hurried out of the shop. He couldn't wait to bring this information to his wife. Soon the news was all over town. Everywhere, people were whispering: "Our rabbi was seen stealing . . . our rabbi is a thief. . . ."

A few days later, the gossip had already found its way back to Yonkel's shop. Two men were standing and talking while waiting for their clothes.

"The rabbi is a real crook," one of them was saying. "Maybe he should leave town."

"Yes. This is an honest community. Something must be done."

Yonkel overheard the men talking, and felt terrible. He decided to visit the rabbi.

Yonkel entered the cramped little study where the rabbi was sitting, looking very depressed. By this time he, too, had heard the rumors being spread about him. The apple seller had given him a present of two apples, and now everyone in town was calling him a thief. How did all this happen?

Are you busy, Rabbi?" Yonkel asked.

"Yonkel, what are you doing here?"

"Rabbi, I have a terrible confession to make. I've been telling a tale about you. I'm really sorry and I beg your forgiveness. I'll tell my customers that the story wasn't true. Will you ever forgive me?" Yonkel cried to the rabbi.

The rabbi thought for a moment and then responded. "Before I can forgive you, go and take several feather pillows from your home. Cut them open and let the feathers fly away."

Yonkel immediately went home and did what the rabbi requested. An hour later he returned to the rabbi.

"I've done exactly what you requested. Now will you forgive me?"

"Not yet," the rabbi answered. "You must do one more thing. Go and gather all the feathers that were scattered by the wind."

"But, but . . . that's impossible," argued Yonkel.

"Precisely," replied the rabbi. "Just as you cannot know where all the feathers have flown, so you can never know where all the rumors have gone. Words fly just like feathers, Yonkel. And just as you can never gather up all the feathers, you can never take back all the things you said about me. So as truly sorry as you may be for what you did, and even though I forgive you, the damage cannot be undone.

- *How badly did Yonkel hurt the rabbi?*
- *Explain how gossiping is like scattering feathers to the wind.*
- *Would it be possible for Yonkel to reach everyone who had heard the gossip about the rabbi and tell them the truth? And will those whom he does reach believe him?*

The power of words

"If you see that someone is sad and dejected, it is a great *mitzvah* to boost his spirits by conversing with him." These words were written by the Hafetz Hayim, a great rabbi who lived in Lithuania between 1838 and 1933. Like other great rabbis before him, he understood the immense power of words to do good and to destroy. And so he devoted his life to teaching Jews how to be careful with their words.

Words are one of the most powerful forces in the world. They can do great good or do terrible harm. They can give comfort and lead people to do good things, or they can cause great hurt and lead people to do horrible things.

Since words have such power, Judaism has always been very concerned with how people use language. The rabbis developed a special term to refer to the destructive use of words. They called it **lashon ha-ra**.

The Hebrew word *lashon* means "language"; *ha-ra* means "the wicked." The two words together mean "language of the wicked." Any use of language that hurts other people—such as name-calling, spreading rumors, or talking behind someone's back—is an example of *lashon ha-ra*.

"Do not go gossiping among your people"

The first *mitzvah* against *lashon ha-ra*, "Do not go gossiping among your people," is in the Torah, in the Book of Leviticus. On the basis of this law, the rabbis of the Talmud and later rabbis developed additional *mitzvot* and guidelines concerning *lashon ha-ra*.

The first level: the gossiper

The first level of *lashon ha-ra* is simple gossip. Here is how Maimonides defined gossip in the *Mishneh Torah*:

"Who is a gossiper? One who carries gossip from person to person, saying, 'So-and-so said this, I have heard such-and-such about so-and-so.'"

Does that sound familiar? It is very likely that you have gossiped. Everyone does at one time or another; most people do it very often. Most people believe that gossip is a harmless form of entertainment. They enjoy telling and hearing stories about others, without realizing how much damage they may be causing.

The second level: the scandal-monger

But gossip is only the beginning of *lashon ha-ra*. Usually people gossip to entertain themselves. They may be thoughtless and inconsiderate, but they are not trying to hurt others. On the other hand, sometimes a person will gossip maliciously, trying to cause harm. Such a person, called a "scandal-monger" by Maimonides, does not just tell stories about people. This person goes around telling bad things about people.

The scandal-monger's stories may be true, but that is beside the point. The point is that these stories do terrible harm. Every person has both good and bad qualities; why then does the scandal-monger talk only about the negative? Probably because he wants to hurt the other person. When people hear bad things about someone—even if they also hear good things—they tend to remember the bad things and continue to think of the person in a negative light.

Because the tales of the scandal-monger can cause so much lasting damage, Maimonides wrote that spreading negative stories about a person is much worse than normal gossip. But there is an even worse form of *lashon ha-ra*.

The third and lowest level: the slanderer

"The one who speaks badly about his neighbor by telling a lie is called a slanderer," explained Maimonides. Slander, or telling lies to destroy another person's name, is the worst form of *lashon ha-ra*.

Slander is extremely harmful. In fact the Talmud says that the tongue, when it slanders, is even more dangerous than a sword. Why? There are three reasons.

First, like the sword, slanderous words can ruin a person's life. But slander also ruins a person's name and reputation.

Second, it is often more difficult to fight against lies than to fight against a sword. When you are attacked by a sword, you usually know that you are being attacked and who is attacking you. But when you are attacked by slander, you usually do not know what is being said to attack you or when you are being attacked. You may not know who is attacking you or even that you are being attacked at all until it is too late. There is almost no way that a person can fight back against a slanderous attack.

Third, a sword wound can heal, but the wounds inflicted by words cannot be healed. Yonkel the tailor wanted to undo the damage he had done to the rabbi. But just as he could never get back all the feathers scattered by the wind, he could never take back all the lies that he had spread. *Lashon ha-ra* can cause permanent damage.

Because slander can ruin a person's life, it is considered the worst form of *lashon ha-ra*.

If lashon ha-ra is so bad, why do people do it so much?

There are many reasons why people speak *lashon ha-ra*. Two of the most common reasons are anger and the desire to be popular.

Suppose one day a friend does something that makes you very angry. That night, in anger, you tell three of your classmates bad things about your friend. The next day, you speak with your friend, and after talking things over, you make up with each other. Even though you are friends again, you may have hurt him permanently. It is often impossible to take back the words you spoke in anger.

A Jewish proverb says, "An angry man opens his mouth and shuts his eyes." When a person gets angry, he is likely to shut his eyes to the consequences of the *lashon ha-ra* he is speaking.

Another reason people gossip is their desire to be popular. Everyone wants to be liked and accepted by others. When a group of people get together, the conversation is often about others. In order to feel included, you will be very tempted to add your own information or opinion about those other people. Gossiping becomes a way for some people to try to become more popular.

When you speak *lashon ha-ra* you often reveal more about yourself than about the person of whom you are speaking.

How to avoid lashon ha-ra

Perhaps the most difficult thing to control is speech. Most people say whatever comes into their minds. But once you begin to understand how powerful words are and how they can destroy others, you will understand why Judaism places such importance on avoiding *lashon ha-ra*. There are many *mitzvot* connected with *lashon ha-ra*, and rabbis have said that if all people observed these laws, the world would be almost ideal.

Hillel's rule can be applied to *lashon ha-ra*: "Do not discuss things about others that you would not like discussed about you." Imagine that a group of your friends are gossiping about someone's parents who are getting a divorce. What if they were your parents—would you like them to be the topic of conversation? If such a discussion would hurt you, then you should realize that it would probably hurt someone else. By putting yourself in another's place, you can find the strength to turn away from *lashon ha-ra*. Perhaps the best way to train yourself to avoid *lashon ha-ra* is to imagine that the person being talked about can hear what is being said.

If you are not speaking *lashon ha-ra*, but people around you are, is it wrong to listen? Yes, it is wrong to listen to *lashon ha-ra* for three basic reasons. First, speakers need listeners. When you listen to *lashon ha-ra*, you are encouraging someone to speak it. Second, when you listen to *lashon ha-ra*, you are allowing yourself to be influenced by what you hear. Third, you will one day be tempted to repeat the *lashon ha-ra* that you heard.

To avoid hearing *lashon ha-ra*, the following is suggested. If you are in a group that begins gossiping, you can excuse yourself and leave the group. Or you can change the subject. And sometimes the best thing to do is the hardest: break into the conversation and say "I don't want to hear you putting other people down."

This may not make you popular at that moment, but it will certainly earn you respect and admiration. Over time, some people may even begin to see you as an example of a good person, and try to act more like you. And you will like yourself more for having been a better person and not participated in putting someone down.

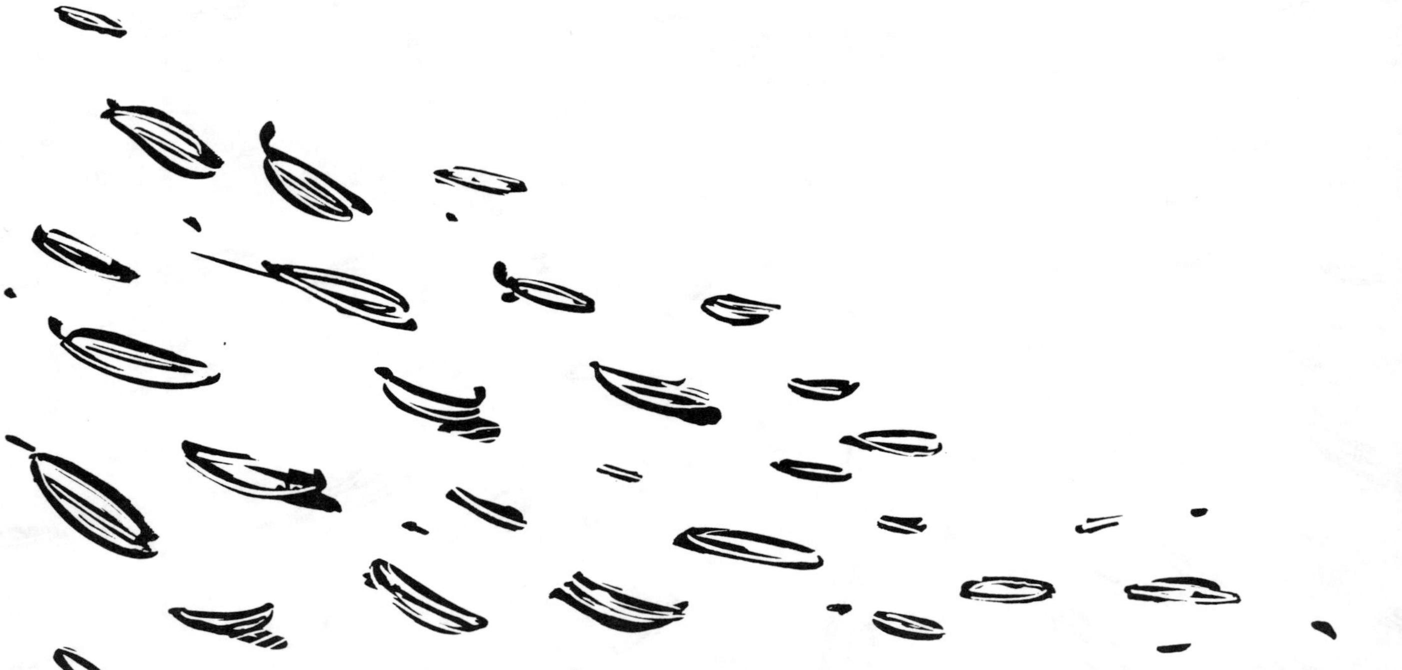

PART FOUR
Mitzvot Between People and God

Food for Thought

Mona Dechalet, the new French ambassador, had just arrived in Washington, D.C. As she and her husband, Pierre, stepped off the plane, they were met by Alex Wagner of the State Department.

"I've been assigned to show you around town," Alex said. "I think you'll love Washington —it's a very exciting city."

"Fine," said the ambassador. "When do we start?"

"Well, why don't you take the afternoon to unwind, and I'll pick you up tonight at around 8:30. We'll go to the finest restaurant in the capitol."

As soon as the French ambassador, her husband, and Alex arrived at La Cuisine, they were greeted by the headwaiter who promptly escorted them to "the best table in the house."

"The service here is excellent, Alex," the ambassador commented after they had ordered dinner.

"Just wait, Madam Ambassador. The food is even better."

Just as Alex had promised, the dinner was superb. And over coffee and delicious French pastries, Mona Dechalet thanked her American host.

"Thanks so much, Alex. The food was as exceptional as at our favorite restaurant in Paris."

"It was truly my pleasure. But I'm not the one to be thanked," Alex replied. "We should all thank the genius in the kitchen."

So Alex called the headwaiter and asked if they could see the chef. Soon the chef, a large figure in white hat and apron, came out.

"Your kind words to me are most appreciated," the chef said to the three guests at the table. "But I am not the one to thank. Do you really want to thank the one responsible for this meal?"

Around the table, three heads nodded in agreement.

"Then come with me in about a half hour, when the restaurant closes. We will all go to the vegetable market."

"Wonderful," exclaimed Alex. "We can all go in the State Department limousine." Seeing everyone's excitement, the headwaiter asked if he, too, could come along. And now there were five people, all in high spirits, driving to the vegetable market. At the outskirts of the city, they stopped at a large produce stand.

"I want you to meet my friend, Joe," said the chef. "He is the one who provides me with the fruit and vegetables that you so enjoyed. This man works harder than anyone else in the business to get the freshest fruit and the tastiest vegetables. Joe, these good people want to thank you."

"That's right," said Alex. "The chef says that you're responsible for the delicious meal we all enjoyed tonight."

"Not me," Joe said. "If you really want to know who's responsible, then I can take you to see another man —he's the one you ought to be thanking. I'll take you to him if you want, but we'll have to drive most of the night to get there."

"Let's go," said the ambassador. "This is fun. I never dreamed Americans have such wild and entertaining evenings."

The group, now including Joe, the chef, the headwaiter, Alex, Mona, and Pierre, piled into the limo and drove into the quiet darkness of farm country. By the time they arrived at Arthur's Vegetable Farm, the first light of dawn was warming the fields.

"What a beautiful country!" Mona whispered to her husband.

"C'mon gang," Joe said. "Let's go meet Arthur, the farmer."

The group walked towards the farmhouse. But they were stopped by what they saw through the open window. The farmer and his family were sitting around a table. "Have you all washed your hands?" the farmer was asking. "Good. Then Jonathan, please lead us in the blessing."

"OK, Dad," said a little boy, about seven years old. "Thank you, God, for giving us these fruits and vegetables and this fine breakfast. Amen."

The farmer lifted his head. He saw the group standing outside the window. "Joe!" he said "What are you doing here so early in the morning? And who are all these people with you?"

Six people stood there, silently, watching the farmer and his family. Not one of them could speak. Finally, Alex broke the silence.

"We had come here to thank you for providing the delicious fruits and vegetables that went into our meal last night at La Cuisine. But now I think we all see things in a different way."

"Yes," said the ambassador. "This great country has courteous waiters, skilled chefs, fine produce buyers and talented farmers. But now we realize that none of them is really responsible for the delicious dinner we had last night."

QUESTIONS FOR DISCUSSION
* *Who really provided the fruit and vegetables? Why is it important to know the answer?*
* *What was the biggest difference between those who ate at the restaurant and those who ate at the farm table?*

Beyn adam la-Makom mitzvot

Jewish laws fall into two categories:

1. **Beyn adam l'ḥavero mitzvot**: Laws concerning relationships between people.
2. **Beyn adam la-Makom mitzvot**: Laws concerning a person's relationship to God.

The purpose of the *beyn adam la-Makom mitzvot* is to bring Jews closer to God. Why do people need such laws?

People are biologically similar to animals and therefore can, and often do, behave like animals. Take eating, for example. When food is put in front of an animal, it gobbles it up quickly. No animal says a blessing before eating or cares about how neatly or sloppily it eats. Animals eat whenever they want, whatever they want, however they want, and all they want. It is natural for people to eat this way, too.

Judaism, through its *beyn adam la-Makom* laws, tries to separate and raise people's actions from those of animals. Therefore, to take eating as an example, there are many *mitzvot* that do not allow Jews to eat like animals. Jews cannot eat whenever and whatever they want. For example, there are fast days when Jews do not eat, and there are some foods which Jews are forbidden to eat. Jews cannot eat however they want; first they must wash and say a blessing. Further, Jews are supposed to eat in moderation.

The *beyn adam la-Makom mitzvot* command Jews to think about God and give thanks for their food before and after eating. In this way, the laws try to raise Jews' behavior to a higher level and bring them as close to God as possible.

The major purpose of the *beyn adam la-Makom mitzvot* is to raise people's actions from the animal-like to the God-like.

Kidushah

Beyn adam la-Makom mitzvot also teach the Jew how to come closer to God.

The complex idea of coming closer to God is called **kidushah** in Hebrew. **Kadosh** means separate or special: to act *kadosh* is to raise you life to a higher level. If you act in a kind, just and compassionate way, and you try to raise all your actions to a God-like level, you will bring *kidushah* or "specialness" into your life.

Kidushah is usually translated as holiness. A more understandable definition might be raising yourself to a higher level by making your actions special and closer to God.

Some Jews do nothing to raise their lives to a higher level. While these Jews are not necessarily evil or criminal, they do not have *kidushah* in their lives. Such individuals might spend a great deal of time worrying about such things as what car they should buy or how they look. Or they might be more concerned with which restaurant to go to than with being kind and acting *kadosh*.

It takes a lot of effort to move closer to God. You cannot do it overnight. Instead, you have to set out on this lifelong journey with small, gradual steps. And you have to work daily at bringing *kidushah* into your life.

The *beyn adam la-Makom mitzvot* are the guidelines. Some of these *mitzvot* raise ordinary actions of daily life—such as eating and waking up in the morning—to acts of *kidushah*. Other *mitzvot* make time *kadosh* by raising ordinary days to Shabbat, holidays, and celebrations. And still others raise words to *kidushah* and guide the Jew in prayer, a time for thinking about God and making yourself a better person.

Kidushah in acts of daily life: the brachah

From the moment they awake in the morning, Jews are commanded to create *kidushah* in their lives. For example, instead of just rolling out of bed and stumbling into the bathroom, the Jew is supposed to start the day by reciting the *modeh ani*. The *modeh ani* is a prayer which begins: "I am grateful to you God for waking me to another day and for renewing my energy and my life."

The *modeh ani* is similar to a **brachah**. A *brachah* blesses God and reminds the Jew that even in the most ordinary acts, such as waking up in the morning, God is present.

The root of the word *brachah* is the Hebrew word for knee. It expresses the idea, "I bend my knees and bow down to welcome You [God], praise You, and give You respect." Every *brachah* refers to God as *Melech ha olam*, King of the universe, and is recited before several daily acts, such as eating and washing the hands.

It is also said before doing certain *mitzvot*. That is why many *brachot* contain the phrase *kid'shanu b'mitzvotav*. *Kid'shanu* means "made us [Jews] *kadosh* [special and holy]," and *b'mitzvotav* means "through God's *mitzvot*." *Brachot* that are recited before doing a *mitzvah* begin, therefore, with "Bless you, God, King of the universe, who made us [Jews] *kadosh* [special] through your *mitzvot*."

You can see how a *brachah* works in the example of eating. An animal eats without thought or awareness. People often eat in the same thoughtless manner. But when Jews eat, and recite *brachot* both before and after the meal, they cannot help but remember that their food comes from God, the Creator of the universe. By reciting a *brachah*, the Jew raises the act of eating to a higher level.

A *brachah* praises God and raises an ordinary act to a higher level.

Food for thought

Alex, Pierre, and Mona enjoyed a delicious and elegant meal at La Cuisine. They did not eat like animals, but neither did they eat with *kidushah*. For all their good manners and their desire to thank the chef, they simply did not have an awareness of God.

In contrast, the farmer's family ate a very simple meal in very plain surroundings. They were not wearing suits and evening gowns; they were not using one fork for salad and another fork for meat. But they gave thought to the act of eating, stopping to thank God for their food. They showed an awareness of God. By Jewish standards, the simple farm breakfast was eaten at a much higher level than the fancy French dinner at La Cuisine.

Coming closer to God

Not only Jews, but all people can come closer to God. All people can be kind, compassionate and just. And when they do so for the sake of God, whether they are Jews or members of other religions, they are coming closer to God. Mother Theresa, a Catholic nun who has spent her life helping starving people in India, is one such individual. Dietrich Bonhoeffer, a Protestant minister who was executed because of his opposition to the Nazis during World War II, and Yosef Mendelevich, a Jew who spent eleven years in a Soviet prison camp because of his fight for human rights, are two other individuals who have raised their lives to a higher level.

While all people can reach a higher level, the *beyn adam la-Makom mitzvot* give Jews a unique way to come closer to God in all their actions. To make the Jews into a good and compassionate people, Judaism gives them the *beyn adam l'ḥavero mitzvot*. And to become a *kadosh* or special people, Judaism has given the Jews the *beyn adam la-Makom mitzvot*. Only by observing both these categories of *mitzvot* can the Jewish people achieve their goal: to be "a light to other nations," an example for others to follow.

CHAPTER 14

Thank God It's Friday

Julie Cohen and Nancy Sternbach have been friends for a long time. They are both Jewish and both thirteen years old, and they have always been in the same class at school. Now in the eighth grade, they still spend lots of time together. Since they like to do the same kinds of things, they usually have no problem deciding where to go, what to do, or whom to see.

Except for Friday nights. That is one night when Julie and Nancy go their separate ways.

At Julie's house, Friday night is very unstructured and no two Friday nights are exactly the same. Her parents usually go out for dinner, leaving Julie and her two brothers to do what they want and to feed themselves. So sometimes they order a pizza, or just grab some leftovers and eat in front of the television, and then listen to the stereo. On other Friday nights, Julie eats out with her friends, and goes with them to a movie, ice skating, or bowling. She usually goes to bed around midnight.

Friday night at Nancy's house is very predictable. For Nancy's family, Friday night means the beginning of Shabbat. They consider Shabbat special, and spend much of Friday afternoon preparing for it. They clean the house and bake ḥallah. They set the dining room table with a white cloth, Shabbat candles, and flowers. Shortly before sundown everyone puts on nice clothes and walks to synagogue. Afterwards, the family gathers around the table, often with one or two guests, to enjoy a long and leisurely meal. They linger most of the evening discussing the week's events, sharing songs, stories, and conversation. After the guests leave, Nancy and her family spend a few quiet moments together. Then, around midnight, Nancy goes to bed.

• *What do you like about Julie's Friday nights? What do you dislike?*
• *What do you like about Nancy's Friday nights? What do you dislike?*
• *Which of these Friday nights would you choose to have every week?*

Making certain days special and meaningful

Some of the *beyn adam la-Makom mitzvot* regulate ordinary, day-to-day acts such as eating and waking up in the morning. They bring *kidushah* into the everyday actions of the Jews who observe them. But there are other *beyn adam la-Makom mitzvot* that go beyond the scope of everyday activities. These *mitzvot* bring *kidushah* into life at special times. They make certain days *kadosh* and connected to God.

What makes a day special? Think about what happens on your birthday. You receive presents, cards, and phone calls from family and friends; you celebrate the day with a party and a cake. If none of these things happened, the day would still be your birthday, but it just wouldn't seem as special. The special actions—the gifts and cards, the party and cake—are what make the day so special.

Jewish holidays are special in the same way, not only because of what happened on those dates, but also because of the special things that Jews do to celebrate. And these days can be made even more than special: through observing the special *mitzvot* of that day, they can be made *kadosh*.

Compare, for example, New Year's Eve and Rosh Hashanah, the Jewish New Year. Both of these holidays mark the beginning of a new year, but they are celebrated in very different ways.

People usually celebrate New Year's Eve by partying, eating and drinking late into the night. For many people, the meaning of New Year's Eve is to have as much fun as possible. Rosh Hashanah is also celebrated with good food and wine, and it is a very enjoyable holiday. But that is not its meaning.

Its meaning is to connect Jews to God, and that is how many Jews observe it. In addition to sitting with their family and friends at special holiday meals, they go to synagogue and reflect on their behavior during the previous year. They ask forgiveness for wrongdoing, and they think about how they can become better people in the coming year. Both New Year's Eve and Rosh Hashanah are special, but only Rosh Hashanah is filled with *kidushah*.

The mitzvot bring kidushah to Jewish holidays

Jews remember important past events and their meaning by celebrating them as special days of *kidushah*, holidays. For example, the holiday of Pesach (Passover) celebrates the time when Jews gained their freedom from Egyptian slavery. Just as you celebrate your birthday with special activities, Jews celebrate Pesach and connect it to God—make it *kadosh*—through special activities. The Pesach *mitzvot* include the Seder, a special dinner when Jews read the Haggadah and re-enact the story of leaving Egypt. At the Seder, Jews eat symbolic foods such as matzah (reminding them of leaving Egypt in a hurry), and sing many songs blessing God.

Shabbat

The story at the beginning of the chapter is about two girls and their different Friday nights. Julie's Friday night was special because she was free to do what she wanted. She didn't have to worry about anyone else in her family; she was left alone. She could stay up late and spend her evening in whatever way she pleased.

Nancy's Friday night was special in another way: it was filled with *kidushah*. She began it with her family and friends at a relaxed Shabbat dinner. Instead of going off in separate directions, the members of the family stay together, discussing things that are important to them and growing closer to each other.

By observing Shabbat *mitzvot* such as singing Shabbat melodies, eating the challah, making the Shabbat *kiddush* (*bracha*) over the wine, and lighting the Shabbat candles, they set Friday night apart from every other day of the week. And by not doing the non-*kadosh* things that they do on other days, like working, watching television, or even ice skating and going to the movies, they make every Friday evening a truly unique experience—of *kidushah*. *Kidushah* transforms Friday night and Saturday into Shabbat.

Shabbat is very important in bringing *kidushah* into Jews lives. It is commanded more times in the Torah than any other *mitzvah*.

Life cycle events

A holiday is one kind of special day. It comes every year, at the same time, and for everyone. There is another type of special day that comes much less frequently, perhaps only once in a lifetime, and is celebrated only by an individual, family and friends. These are the events that introduce big changes into people's lives. Some examples are the birth of a child, becoming a Bar Mitzvah, or getting married. The *beyn adam la-Makom mitzvot* provide guidelines for making these life cycle events *kadosh*.

When a girl is born, a beautiful ceremony is held in which the baby is named and welcomed into the Jewish people. And an eight-day-old boy is circumcised at a *Brit Milah*. The community comes to these events to recite *brachot*, eat a festive meal, and share in the celebration.

Of course, some life cycle events are not happy. But here, too, Judaism provides *mitzvot*. And by observing these special *mitzvot*, Jews have always been able to get through difficult times, such as the death of a loved one, illness, or misfortune. The *mitzvot* allow people to accept painful events by providing a structure that helps them feel closer to others and closer to God.

Spiritual rewards

Observing the *beyn adam la-Makom mitzvot* makes a Jew's life richer, more meaningful, and more connected to God. The word "richer" does not refer to physical rewards that you can see or touch, like a new bicycle or a ten-dollar bill. What the *mitzvot* can bring you are spiritual rewards—the kind that you cannot see but that fill your thoughts with meaning and raise the quality of your life. Many Jews who observe *mitzvot* say their lives are filled with contentment and inner happiness. And they speak of a deeper connection to God as a result of practicing *mitzvot*.

Nancy was not able to do everything that Judy could do on a Friday night. She would have to wait until Saturday night or some other night to go ice skating or to the movies. But she enjoyed something better: Shabbat. "Fun" things like watching TV or going out for pizza are usually forgotten almost the minute they are over. But the warm feeling left by Shabbat lasts the whole week long. And the next Shabbat is looked forward to all week long. When you observe Shabbat with your family, you experience spiritual and family rewards and a more enjoyable, meaningful life.

Shabbat is one of the special days with which Judaism fills life with *kidushah* and brings people closer to God—and to each other.

Who Said You Can't Teach an Old Horse New Tricks?

Susan was already at her desk when Eddie came into the classroom. He took his usual seat next to her and smiled.

"Hi, Eddie," she said. "What are you so happy about?"

"About spring vacation. I'm going to Colorado to visit my cousin. He has a ranch with twenty horses! And he says I'll be able to train my own horse and ride him every day!"

"That sounds great," said Susan.

"Yeah, I'm so excited I can hardly sleep at night or pay attention in class."

"I hope you can pay attention in my class, Eddie," a man's voice said suddenly. It was Cantor Glickman, who had just entered the room.

"OK, class, let's begin where we left off last week. Open your books to page 231. We'll start by studying the meaning of the Haftarah blessings, and then we'll read them together."

After half an hour of study, the class began reading in unison, "Baruch Atah . . . Melech ha-olam. . . ."

Eddie started along with the rest of the class, but soon he began thinking about his Colorado vacation, and the Hebrew words seemed far, far away. He closed his eyes for a moment, and when he opened them, he found himself walking down an unfamiliar country road. He took a deep breath, enjoying the crisp mountain air and the cool tingly scent of a pine forest.

At the sound of hoofbeats he turned to see a horse and rider coming swiftly up the road. Eddie took a closer look, and saw that the rider looked a lot like Cantor Glickman.

"Howdy Eddie! Welcome to Colorado!"

Eddie was so amazed, he could barely speak. "How did you know my name?" he finally managed to say. "Who are you?"

"Don't you know who I am?" the rider asked. "I am Moshe the Magician. Hop on my horse and come with me."

"But I can't. I'm on my way to my cousin's ranch. I'll be able to train my own horse, there."

"But Moshe the Magician has the best horse ranch in these parts. And I can train a horse to do anything. Let me show you my place, Eddie. If you still want to go to your cousin's, I'll take you there afterwards."

Eddie thought a moment. "OK, it's a deal." He climbed up on the magician's horse. Minutes later they arrived at a magnificent castle.

"Whoa, boy," the magician said to his horse. Then he turned to Eddie. "Well, pardner, come in and see my horses," Eddie dismounted and followed the magician through the castle door. They entered a huge stable with hundreds of prancing white horses.

"Wow," Eddie said, "this is fantastic. Nobody back home will ever believe it!"

"And now, I'll show you a very special horse. I trained him with you in mind." The magician led Eddie to another set of stables, just as large as the first. But here there was only one horse —the most elegant and graceful animal he had ever seen. The horse had a kippah on his head and a tallit thrown over his mane.

"Wow!" said Eddie. "He's beautiful."

"And well trained, too. Watch this, Eddie —I've taught him to pray!"

"Pray! But that's impossible. No horse can pray."

The magician took a Siddur from a shelf. He opened it and

placed it on a low table in front of the horse. Then he reached into a feedbag, took a handful of oats, and scattered them across the open Siddur. He took some more oats and sprinkled them between the pages of the rest of the book.

The horse stuck his head into the Siddur and began to eat. When he finished all the oats on that page, he used his wet nose to flick the page and reach the next pile of food.

"That's a pretty good trick," said Eddie. "But he's not really praying."

"What do you mean, he isn't praying?" Moshe the Magician put his arm around Eddie. "Why, look, he can even turn the page . . . turn the page . . . turn the page. . . ."

"Turn the page, Eddie. It's your turn to recite the Haftarah blessings." Cantor Glickman had placed a hand on Eddie's shoulder and was waiting for him to begin.

QUESTIONS FOR DISCUSSION
- *Was the horse really praying? Why or why not?*
- *With enough training, could a horse learn to pray? What about a monkey? A parrot? Any animal? Why or why not?*
- *What is the difference between the students learning how to pray and the horse's learning how to pray?*
- *What do you think is the purpose of prayer?*

Tefillah is not only prayer

The *beyn adam la-Makom mitzvot* are the laws concerned with people's relationship to God. They bring *kidushah* into acts of daily life and make certain days *kadosh*.

Another area of the *beyn adam la-Makom mitzvot* is prayer.

Have you ever found yourself in a synagogue going through the motions, but not really understanding the meaning or purpose of your prayers? People often feel this way, because they usually do not understand what prayer is all about.

In fact, the word prayer is very misleading. When people think of prayer, they usually think of asking God for things or just reciting praises of God. Jewish prayer is much more than this. Prayer is, in fact, an incomplete translation of the Hebrew word, **tefillah**, which also means "judging." Therefore when you **mitpallel** (pray), you are also judging yourself—your motivations, intentions, and actions—your whole life.

Everyone has some behavior or attitude that needs improvement. A major reason for setting aside time for *tefillah* is to set aside time for self-judgment.

Tefillah as self-judgment before God

The book which contains the *tefillot* (prayers) is the **Siddur**. Open a Siddur and you will find that almost every *tefillah* contains words of praise for God. What is the relationship between praising God and judging yourself? Why bother praising God at all? Does God need to be constantly reminded of God's great qualities?

First, it is very important to understand that people praise God not because God needs their praises, but because people need to praise God. It is extremely important for people to remind themselves that they are not the highest things in the world. Because you are reminded during *tefillah* that there is something higher, you are more likely to remember that you are not the center of the universe and there is a lot that you can do to improve yourself.

Praising God during *tefillah* reminds Jews that God is higher than them. This idea of humility before God is extremely important in Judaism, and indeed in nearly all religions. This is the reason, for example, for the *kippah*, or *yarmulka*: wearing a covering on the head is supposed to be a reminder that there is something higher, something above.

Second, in order to judge yourself you need to measure yourself against a higher standard. Praising God's great qualities during *tefillah* reminds you of the higher standards against which you should judge yourself.

Third, *tefillah* reminds you to think about God and the *mitzvot*. This, too, is very important in helping you judge yourself and become a better person. Many *tefillot* remind Jews to observe the *mitzvot*. Thus, for example, if you have been disrespectful to your parents, the *tefillah* reminds you that you are commanded by God to honor your father and mother. By remembering God and the *mitzvot* you will know that you are wrong in being disrespectful and therefore, you will work on improving the situation with your parents.

Here are some examples of tefillot:

1. *"Listen people of Israel, the Lord is our God, the Lord is one."* This *tefillah*, the **Shema**, expresses the central idea in Judaism: there is one God, who is the highest authority in the universe. This *tefillah* reminds Jews to recognize one God.

2. *"Blessed are you God, King of the universe, who chose us from all other people and gave us the Torah."* This *tefillah*, recited before reading the Torah, reminds Jews that they have been chosen for the task of making the world better through Judaism. Because they have been chosen, Jews must constantly ask themselves: *"How am I fulfilling the Jewish task to make this world better?"*

Tefillah as gratitude

A man needed a telephone number. Since he didn't have a phone book, he called Directory Assistance. To his surprise, a talking computer answered. The computer responded properly to all his questions. The man wanted to thank the computer for all its help, but felt ridiculous saying "thank you" to a computer. At first it bothered him that he could not express his gratitude. But after using the service a few more times, he no longer felt the need.

It is very easy in life to take everything we have for granted. *Tefillot* give people an opportunity to recognize and appreciate all the good things in their lives. Perhaps without this opportunity to express thanks, people would become spoiled, and stop feeling any appreciation for the good things that God has given them.

Most *tefillot* do not ask God for wishes or favors. Instead, they express gratitude to God. And just as God does not need people's praises, neither does God need people's expressions of thanks. But people do need to express thanks, or they will become ungrateful and unappreciative.

Here is an example of a *tefillah* that expresses gratitude. "Blessed are you, God, King of the universe, who gave us life, and raised us up, and brought us to this time."

This *tefillah*, known as the **Shehehiyanu**, is recited at special times in a Jew's life. Jews say the *Shehehiyanu* whenever they wish to celebrate the specialness of a particular moment, like the start of a holiday, the beginning of a new season, or a happy personal occasion. Some people say this blessing before the first taste of a new fruit in season, or when they take their first trip to Israel. In reciting the *Shehehiyanu*, Jews express their thanks to God for allowing them to reach an important moment in their lives.

Tefillah as coming closer to God

Tefillah has the same purpose as all the other *beyn adam la-Makom mitzvot*: to bring Jews closer to God and to bring *kidushah* into their lives. How does *tefillah* do this? By giving Jews a way to express gratitude, to reach out to God, and to judge themselves by God's standards. Through *tefillah* you can come closer to God.

Obtaining *kidushah* through *tefillah* is not an easy task; it requires much discipline and determination. A certain atmosphere is needed. To achieve this, there are special *mitzvot* concerning *tefillah*. Three times a day, Jews are instructed to say *tefillot*: *shacharit* (morning), *minchah* (afternoon), and *ma'ariv* (evening).

While a Jew may say *tefillot* alone, it is always preferable that *tefillah* take place in a group. There are even some *tefillot* which may not be recited unless a **minyan**—a minumum of ten—is present. The experience of *tefillah* is much more powerful when a community gathers together to recite to God their beliefs and praises. Most people enjoy the warmth, support, and sense of belonging that comes from saying *tefillot* in a group.

This idea of community is extremely important in *tefillah* for yet another reason. The Jew is supposed to pray for everyone, not just for himself. That is why you will almost never find the word "I" in any *tefillah*. Nearly every *tefillah* uses "we" instead of "I." In the **Amidah** prayer, for example, Jews pray, "Heal *us*," not "Heal *me*."

Tefillah is more than going through the motions

Moshe the Magician claimed that his horse could pray. But, of course, the horse was only going through the motions of prayer. He could stick his nose into a Siddur and even turn the pages, but he could never judge himself, express gratitude, or experience a feeling of closeness to God. Animals do not have the ability to engage in *tefillah*; only people have this ability.

While people can simply go through the motions of *tefillah* like Moshe the Magician's horse, the most meaningful *tefillah* takes place when Jews have the right kind of intention and motivation. The Hebrew word for this intention is **kavannah**. If you say *tefillot* with *kavannah*, you are sincere in your intention to express thanks, to judge yourself, and to feel a personal connection to God. *Kavannah* and *tefillah* go together.

What if you don't have *kavannah* — is there still a value in saying *tefillot*? Yes. Even a Jew who says *tefillot* without *kavannah* can get something out of it. Even by going through the motions of *tefillah*, you are putting yourself into an atmosphere of *kidushah*, and are giving yourself the chance to develop *kavannah*. Judaism recognizes that people always have the potential to grow and to change, and by regularly saying *tefillot*, any Jew may develop *kavannah* and eventually come closer to God.

A Flight to Remember

The plane had taken off smoothly. The pilot removed the Fasten Seatbelts sign and the passengers began roaming up and down the aisle. In his window seat, Jeff Hansen looked at his watch and settled back to read his newspaper, satisfied that he would arrive on schedule. Within minutes, the voice of the flight attendant could be heard throughout the cabin.

"Ladies and gentlemen, at this time we will begin serving dinner. We would like to ask you to take your seats, to make it easier for us to move the food cart down the aisle."

The man in the seat next to Jeff seemed pleased. "Great," he said, "I was getting pretty hungry."

"So was I," Jeff said. "Well, it won't be long now."

The flight attendant made another announcement. "Ladies and gentlemen, at this time we would like all those passengers who have ordered special meals to identify themselves. Please signal us on your call button when you hear your name. Mr. Jeff Hansen. . . ."

Upon hearing his name, Jeff pressed the call button.

"So your name's Jeff Hansen?" his neighbor inquired. "Nice to meet you, Jeff. I'm Rob Sachs."

"Glad to meet you, Rob."

"What kind of special meal did you order?"

"A kosher meal."

"No kidding. You don't really keep kosher, do you?"

"Yes, I . . ."

"You probably ordered it," Rob interrupted, *"because you think that the kosher meals taste better. Actually, this airline serves great food —you should try it."*

"I've heard that the food is good on this airline, Rob. That's not why I ordered a kosher meal. I have different reasons for keeping kosher."

"I'd be interested in hearing them."

"OK, sure."

At that moment the flight attendant arrived with Jeff's kosher meal. As she placed the tray in front of him, she said, *"I hope you don't mind my asking, sir, but I'm very curious. What exactly is kosher food? Is it food that's been blessed by a rabbi?"*

Before Jeff could answer, Rob began to speak. *"Kosher food is not food that has been blessed,"* he said, *"it's food that is cleaner, healthier, and tastier. In the days before refrigeration, Jews preserved meat with kosher salt. And they were prohibited from eating animals, like the pig, that carried diseases. By keeping kosher, Jews kept themselves healthier than the other people around them. Today, of course, with refrigeration and government controls over meat, keeping kosher is not really necessary. But a lot of people still do, so I guess it's because they like the tradition."*

Jeff had been sitting with a slight frown on his face. Now he broke his silence.

"I'm afraid that neither of you knows why Jews keep kosher. Let me explain it to you."

QUESTIONS FOR DISCUSSION
• *Have you heard any of the explanations for keeping kosher that were presented in the story? Which ones?*
• *What makes food kosher or unkosher?*
• *Can you think of reasons for keeping kosher?*

Kosher means "fitting and proper"

The system of **kashrut**, or "keeping kosher," is one of the most misunderstood of all Jewish practices. While many Jews are familiar with the word "kosher," very few actually know what it means or why it is so important.

The Hebrew word **kasher** means "fitting" or "proper." Food that is *kasher* (or kosher) is food that is fitting or proper for Jews to eat.

How do Jews know what is fitting and proper for them to eat and what is not? There are guidelines about eating throughout the Torah and the Talmud. The earliest Jewish guidelines appear at the start of Genesis, the first book of the Torah.

Vegetarianism —is it the Jewish ideal?

Adam and Eve, the first humans, lived in a paradise called the Garden of Eden, where God provided everything they could ever need. "I give you every seed-bearing plant [vegetables]," God said to them, "and every tree that has seed-bearing fruit. These shall be yours for food."

God instructed Adam and Eve to be vegetarians. They were not permitted to kill animals for food. This idea of not eating meat is repeated in another part of the Bible, in the vision of the prophet Isaiah. The Book of Isaiah describes a future world, a paradise, where no living creature will be eaten by any other. Because the Bible seems to mention the idea of vegetarianism together with the idea of an ideal, perfect world, many Jews believe that vegetarianism represents Judaism's ideal way to eat.

Vegetarianism may or may not be the Jewish ideal. But it is clear that Judaism in no way allows the opposite of vegetarianism—the unrestricted and unlimited killing of animals for food. The Torah and the Talmud are filled with laws about killing animals for food, because Judaism understands that killing—even for food—is a moral problem.

One of the first of these laws can be found in the Book of Genesis. After the great flood, God spoke to Noah, giving people permission to eat meat for the first time, but with one important restriction:

Every creature that lives shall be yours to eat; as with the green grasses. I give you all these. You must not, however, eat flesh with its life-blood in it.

God now allowed people to eat meat, but they could not eat the meat with the animal's blood in it. The blood had to be completely drained from the meat. The Torah explains why. Blood represents the animal's life (fruit and vegetables do not have blood). By removing the blood, people remember that this was a living creature.

In another very early law, God also restricted the way in which people killed animals. The Torah, in Leviticus commands, "You must not tear off a limb from a living animal." God now allowed people to kill animals for food, but also demanded that people not kill them cruelly.

The Torah begins by permitting people to eat only fruits and vegetables. Later, however, it permits people to eat meat, but with restrictions.

The kashrut system

These early laws apply to all people, Jews and non-Jews alike. But the Torah contains other laws about meat eating that apply only to Jews. These are the *mitzvot* of *kashrut*, which like all *mitzvot* are designed to make the Jews a *kadosh* people and a "light to the nations."

The *mitzvot* of *kashrut* have several purposes. They prevent needless cruelty to animals; they help Jews develop a high level of sensitivity to animal life; and they bring *kiddushah* into the everyday act of eating.

The *kashrut* system covers four major areas: (1) *kasher* animals—the animals that Jews are permitted to eat; (2) the *kasher* killing of animals; (3) the prohibition against eating blood; and (4) the separation of milk and meat.

Kasher animals

The *mitzvot* of *kashrut* allow Jews to eat animals, but only certain types of them. The animals that are permitted, or *kasher*, are listed in the Book of Leviticus.

1. *Land animals*. A land animal is *kasher* only if it chews its cud and has split hooves. Any animal that does not have both of these characteristics cannot be eaten. A pig, for example, is not *kasher* only because it does not chew its cud and not, as some people think, because it is dirty or unhealthy.

2. *Birds*. The Torah forbids Jews to eat any bird of prey—a bird that kills other animals for food. That is why the eagle, for example, is not *kasher*. The Torah does permit eating other birds such as turkeys, chickens and ducks.

3. *Fish*. Only those sea animals that have fins and scales are *kasher*. Many fish are *kasher*, but many are not. Sharks, for example, have fins but do not have scales. And shellfish—like lobster, shrimp, crabs, and clams—have neither fins nor scales. They are not *kasher* and Jews are forbidden to eat them.

Out of the thousands of animals that exist in the world, Jews can eat only a few. By limiting the number of animals that can be eaten, the *kashrut* system constantly reminds Jews that their food was once the flesh of a living, breathing animal. *Kashrut* reminds Jews that although they may not be vegetarians now, in Judaism's ideal world no living creature will be eaten by any other.

Of the thousands of animals that exist in the world, the number that Jews may kill and eat is restricted by the *mitzvot* of *kashrut* to just a few.

How kasher animals are to be killed

The *kashrut* system also seeks to have animals suffer as little as possible when they are killed. There are many *mitzvot* regulating the slaughter, or **shehitah**, of animals. For example, Jewish law demands that the killing be done with a sharp knife so the animal dies as quickly and painlessly as possible. A quick and deep slash across the throat cuts the flow of blood to the head, causing the animal to lose consciousness almost immediately. And the knife blade must be completely smooth. If the blade has any nicks, it will tear the flesh more than necessary, so the knife must be carefully examined both before and after each use.

The person who performs the *shehitah* is called a **shohet**. Because the rules of *shehitah* are so complicated, a *shohet* must be trained for a long time before receiving a license to practice *kasher* slaughtering. In addition, the *shohet* must be an observant Jew and a very kind, sensitive person — the type of person who will make every effort to spare the animals any unnecessary pain.

When the rabbis of the Talmud discussed the laws of *shehitah*, they wondered whether or not to include fish. They concluded that the killing of fish does not require *shehitah*. Fish do not have a nervous system nearly as advanced as that of birds and land animals, so they cannot suffer nearly as much. The rabbis did say, however, that since nets cause less pain than hooks, fisherman should use nets whenever possible.

The major purpose of the *shehitah* laws of the *kashrut* system is that animals suffer as little as possible when slaughtered for food.

The prohibition against eating blood

God's warning to Noah is repeated several times throughout the Torah. In the Book of Deuteronomy for example, God says:

> Make sure that you do not eat blood, because blood is the soul and you must not eat the soul with the flesh.

Blood is the source of life for all animals, and therefore a symbol of life itself. Because Jews must always remember that the meat they are eating was once a living animal—it is not just a hamburger or a hot dog—they may not eat meat with its life-blood still in it. The laws of Judaism strictly forbid the eating or drinking of an animal's blood.

The *shoḥet* must "draw out the animal's blood and return it to God." By returning the blood to the earth, and through the earth, to God, Jews remind themselves that the animal's life, like all life, belongs to God.

Blood is the source and symbol of life. Eating of an animal's blood is forbidden.

The separation of milk and meat

"Do not cook a baby lamb in its mother's milk" is a law that appears three times in the Torah. Based on this law, the Talmud forbids Jews from eating milk and meat together.

One purpose of this part of the *kashrut* system is to remind the Jew—yet again—that the meat he or she is eating was once a living animal. Milk represents life—that is how the animal feeds its young. And the meat represents death. By separating meat from milk, the Jew is separating life from death and remembering that the meat is really a dead animal. To remember the living animal that once grew up drinking milk, and then produced milk for its own young, Jews are not to eat meat together with milk.

The Talmudic rabbis debated whether chickens, turkeys, and other birds could be eaten with milk. Unlike mammals, birds do not feed their young with milk. The rabbis considered the fact that the meat of birds, when cooked, resembles the meat of other animals. Therefore, to avoid confusion, the rabbis applied the law of milk and meat separation to chickens, turkeys, and other birds.

Fish do not produce milk and their flesh does not resemble meat. Therefore, according to Jewish law, all *kasher* fish may be eaten with milk.

To help Jews keep milk and meat separate, Jewish law codes give some additional *mitzvot*. For example, Jews should use two sets of cooking and eating utensils, one for milk and one for meat. And after eating meat, Jews must wait a few hours before they can eat any milk products.

Not eating milk with meat represents the separation of life and death and reminds the Jew of the animal's life and death.

Kashrut and kidushah

The purpose of the *mitzvot* is to make the Jewish people moral and *kadosh*. The purpose of the *mitzvot* of *kashrut* is to make the eating of animals moral and *kadosh*.

By keeping the *mitzvot* of *kashrut*, you will remember every time you eat meat that it was once a living animal. Every time you eat — whether in your own home or a friend's, a restaurant or a school cafeteria — you will stop and consider which animal it came from and how the animal was slaughtered. You cannot eat everything that you want. By observing *kashrut*, every time you eat, you will be reminded that you are a Jew, and therefore have a special obligation to be sensitive to animals. When you keep kosher, you raise the act of eating to a higher level, thereby bringing *kidushah* into that part of your life.

Eating is one of the most common activities of human life. Every day, three times a day (sometimes more), people put food into their bodies. The *mitzvot* take this ordinary and frequent activity and turn it into an occasion to come closer to God. This is a main purpose of the laws of *kashrut*, and all the *beyn adam la-Makom mitzvot*. A person who is aware of animal suffering and tries to lessen it, places himself closer to God.

PART FIVE

Belonging to Am Yisrael

CHAPTER 17

How Much Wood Could a Woodchop Chop?

A long time ago, there was a large and powerful kingdom. It was made up of twelve large provinces and many different kinds of people. The country was so huge that people from one end of the land could barely understand the language of people from the other end. A rich and powerful king ruled the kingdom from his capital city. He lived in a big castle surrounded by miles and miles of beautiful woodland.

One day the king decided to build a new castle. He wanted to live in the biggest, most splendid castle ever seen. The time had come, thought the king, to cut down all the trees in the surrounding forests. So he issued a call to all the woodchoppers in the land. They came from every direction, from all twelve provinces of the kingdom. Soon there were hundreds of woodchoppers in the city.

The king wanted the woodchoppers to enjoy their stay. He gave them food and lodging in a luxurious inn. He provided entertainment every night. After each day's work, the woodchoppers would gather in the saloon of the inn for a hearty dinner followed by drinks, music, and dancing. And the king, who enjoyed a good party himself, would often come and join them.

But one evening the king noticed that some of the woodchoppers were missing.

"Where are all the Jewish woodchoppers?" he asked his minister.

"Where are all the Jewish woodchoppers?" his minister asked the chief woodchopper.

"Oh, they all disappear every evening at about this time," the chief woodchopper said.

"Where do they go?" the king demanded.

"We don't know, sire. They always come back in time to do their share of the work, so it never seemed to matter."

The king did not agree. He felt insulted that the Jews should not want to join in all the festivities he had so generously provided. Perhaps they were drinking in some other tavern! Or worse, maybe they were plotting to overthrow the government! So he hired a spy to follow the Jews and find out what they were up to when they disappeared.

The next day, the spy followed the Jews as they left the work area. They walked deep into the forest until they reached a clearing with the remains of a campfire. When they had the fire going again, they sat down in a circle around it.

"Aha!" said the spy to himself. "The king was surely right. They are plotting the overthrow of the government."

But the Jews simply pulled books out of their packs and began reciting the evening prayer. Then they discussed their weekly Torah portion. Afterwards they ate a simple meal of bread and cheese, saying blessings before and after eating.

The spy sat spellbound for several hours, until he could no longer contain his amazement. He broke into the circle and told the Jews who he was.

"You are truly an amazing group," he said. "All the other woodchoppers, tired after a hard day in the forests, stay in the inn, where they can eat and drink as much as they want. But you Jews walk farther into the forest, where you pray and study, and eat a simple meal together. How can this be?"

"We eat together, sir, because we follow specific dietary laws," one of the Jews replied. "As for praying and studying Torah, well, these are also laws that Jews must follow."

"But I still don't understand," protested the spy. "This is a tremendous land, with many different kinds of people and many different traditions. At the inn, the woodchoppers drink and eat only with people from the same province. Yet you Jews, who also come from all twelve provinces of the kingdom, understand each other and spend the evening in each others' company. Is it possible that you Jewish woodchoppers have all met before?"

"No, sir, we never met before the king summoned us to the capital. We simply follow Jewish law and this is what binds us together as a community. If you went to any place in the kingdom, or to any other land in the world, you would find that all the Jews do as we do."

• *What united the Jews from all the different provinces of the kingdom?*
• *Why did the Jewish woodchoppers from different provinces have more in common with each other than with the non-Jewish woodchoppers from their own province?*

The Jewish nation and its homeland

The Jewish people have always been known by their Hebrew name, **Am Yisrael**. The word *am* means nation, and *Yisrael* (Israel) is the name given to the descendants of Jacob. Jacob was the grandson of Abraham, the first Jew, and Jacob's other name was *Yisrael*. After receiving the Torah at Mount Sinai, the people of Israel became a nation with its own religion, Judaism. *Am Yisrael* has always been a nation united by Judaism.

For forty years *Am Yisrael* wandered in the desert. After receiving the Torah at Mount Sinai, Moses, their leader, told them that they would soon enter their homeland, the land of Canaan, promised to them by God. But Moses died before they entered their homeland. Joshua became the new leader of *Am Yisrael*, and led them into the land of Canaan. It eventually became known as Judea, the homeland of the Jewish people, and from which the word "Jew" comes.

The Jews lived in Judea for more than a thousand years. During that time they were conquered twice, and each time they were thrown out of their homeland. After the first conquest and exile to Babylonia, in 586 B.C.E., many of the Jews returned to Judea. But when the Romans put down the Jewish rebellion in 70 C.E., one million Jews died in a war of resistance. Many others were forced to leave their homeland.

They fled in every direction, to many different countries. For the next 1,900 years, up until our own time, Jews have lived in communities all over the world. And yet they have remained *Am Yisrael*: one nation united by a common history, common beliefs and practices, and common responsibility for each other.

In 1948, almost two thousand years after the Roman conquest of Judea, the Jews regained control of their homeland. On May 14, 1948, the Jewish state, Israel, was reborn.

Why did the Jews remain united?

The Jewish woodchoppers came to the capital city from every province. Although they did not know each other before they arrived, they were united by a very strong bond. They were close to each other because they shared the same practices and values. They all observed the same *mitzvot*, connecting them to Jews all over the world.

For nearly two thousand years, *Am Yisrael*, the Jewish nation, was without its homeland. Jews, therefore, have lived throughout the world, with large communities in Europe, the Americas, North Africa, and Asia. And while Jews adopted the languages and many of the customs of their neighbors, they always considered themselves members of the Jewish nation.

As that amazed spy asked the Jewish woodchoppers: How is this possible? How have these communities, spread so far apart for so long, maintained the strong bond of Jewish nationhood?

The answer is that the existence and survival of the Jewish nation was never dependent upon the Jews having their homeland. Rather, the existence and survival of the Jews have always been based on a shared history, shared beliefs and practices, and shared responsibility.

Shared history

When the Jews lived in their homeland, Judea, they had a common history in the same way any nation living in its own land has a common history. But even after the Jews lost their land, they never forgot their common history. They kept their identity as a nation and continued to record their history as a nation, even though they were now living in many different lands. They knew that no matter where they lived, they were still *Am Yisrael*.

Even today, when Jews study their people's history, they study the history of Jews everywhere. American Jews, for example, do not just study when and how certain Jews came to settle in America. They also study the history of Jews in Spain, Italy, Egypt, Russia, and wherever else Jewish history was made.

For almost two thousand years, despite their physical separation from one another, the Jews stayed united as a nation with a common history.

Shared beliefs and practices

Even more than a shared history, it is Judaism that has united Jews. By believing in Judaism, and observing its *mitzvot*, Jews have remained one people. Judaism enables Jews from all over the world to eat, pray, and study in the same way, and then, whenever and wherever Jews can come together, they can, like the woodchoppers in the forests, share everything and feel like one people.

Thus, a Jew from Madrid who keeps kosher will look for and find a home in London where he can eat a kosher meal. A thirteen-year-old Bar Mitzvah in Casablanca, Morocco reads the same Torah portion as a Bar Mitzvah in Las Vegas, Nevada. Jews in Argentina, in Italy, and in North America all have the same Pesach seder on the same evening. And they read the same Hebrew words from the same traditional Haggadah, even though their daily language might be Spanish, Italian, or English. These Jewish practices, based on Jews' shared Jewish beliefs, connect Jews all over the world.

Shared responsibility

The Talmud declares that all Jews are responsible for each other. This shared responsibility reaches beyond the borders of the local community and even extends to Jews in foreign countries. Jews are commanded to care for poor and oppressed Jews everywhere in the world.

For example, one *mitzvah* commands Jews to free any Jew held captive. In the Middle Ages, when Jews were sometimes captured by slave dealers, their communities would raise large amounts of money to pay their ransom. *Mitzvot* such as these have united the Jewish people and directed them to act on behalf of any Jew who needs help.

The *mitzvot* of Jewish mutual responsibility ensure that Jews living in freedom work on behalf of Jews living in countries of oppression. In 1969, for example, Jews around the world received the first messages of distress from Jews in the Soviet Union. These messages revealed that many Soviet Jews were being treated terribly and wanted to leave the Soviet Union for Israel.

Less than one year later, the First World Congress on Soviet Jewry assembled in Brussels, Belgium. Thousands of Jews came from all over the world to discuss the plight of the Soviet Jews, and to develop plans to help them. Since then, more than 250,000 Jews have been able to leave the Soviet Union, thanks to the persistent efforts of Jews in Western countries.

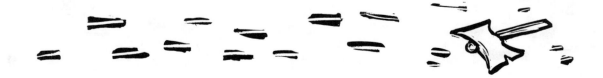

Similarly, Jews work to free oppressed Jews in Ethiopia and Syria and to help poor Jews in places like Morocco and Tunisia. In 1985 an Israeli rescue operation brought thousands of Jews out of Ethiopia into Israel, from oppression to freedom.

These three unique aspects of *Am Yisrael* — common history, common beliefs and practices, and mutual responsibility — enabled the Jewish people to survive even though they did not regain their homeland until May 14, 1948.

Common history, beliefs and practices, and shared responsibilities have kept the Jewish people united throughout history.

CHAPTER 18

A True Story of Courage

This is the true story of a young Jewish woman named Avital. Today she lives in Israel, but once she lived and worked in the Soviet Union.

One morning in Moscow, Avital was on her way to work. She boarded a trolley bus and headed for an empty seat. As she settled down she heard an angry voice coming from the seat behind her.

"What's going on?" a man was saying, "What's all that noise up ahead?"

"It's another one of those Jewish demonstrations," another man answered. "They keep making trouble."

Avital quickly turned and looked out the window. She saw a small group of demonstrators carrying signs. They were surrounded by armed police and tall men in black suits. KGB agents! She watched, horrified, as the police threw the signs onto the ground and began shoving the demonstrators into wagons.

The bus driver increased speed, trying to pass the demonstration as quickly as possible. But Avital kept her eyes glued to the scene. Suddenly she gasped —there was her brother Michael! He was carrying a sign that said "Let us go home to Israel."

She became very frightened. A sign like that was against the law. In the Soviet Union, no one was allowed to express a desire to leave the country. The police would arrest Michael and take him to jail.

Avital ran to the front of the bus, yelling "Let me out! Please open the door!" But the driver ignored her and did not slow down. The last sight she had of her brother and his companions was of the police dragging them away.

Instead of waiting for her usual stop, Avital got off the bus as soon as she could. She ran back to the place where she had last seen her brother. But by the time she got there, the street was empty. There was no sign that there had ever been a demonstration.

Avital didn't know what to do. Throughout the day she kept trying to contact Michael's friends, but none of them were home. Maybe they had all been arrested! Avital returned home exhausted and desperate. She had one last hope. Tomorrow was Shabbat. She would go to the main synagogue of Moscow —maybe someone there would have news about her brother. This was dangerous, she knew, because the secret police were always watching the synagogue, and would be keeping a record of anyone who went near the building. But for the sake of her brother she had to risk it.

Early the next morning Avital went to the synagogue. She was looking around nervously for some of her brother's friends when a young man came up to her.

"You look so upset," the young man said. "What is it?"

"They've arrested my brother," Avital said. She told him what she had seen from the bus window.

"Don't worry, I'm sure he'll be released soon. I myself have just been released after fifteen days in prison."

Avital's new friend introduced himself as Anatoly Scharansky. The two of them stayed together the rest of that afternoon. He told her of his dream —the same as her brother's —to go to the land of Israel. Life was wonderful there, he said. There a Jew could leave in freedom, without the constant fear that Jews feel in the Soviet Union.

He told her that he was a computer specialist who had lost his job when he applied for permission to leave the country. He wanted to go to Israel, but the government would not let him go. The government had also disconnected his telephone and kept him from sending or receiving any mail. He explained that these punishments, and even worse ones, were typical for all Jews who had become refuseniks. A refusenik, he said, is someone who applies to go to Israel but is refused permission.

Avital and Anatoly spent many days together. Before long, they fell in love. They decided to get married and build a new life together in Israel. But the Soviet government still refused to give them permission to leave. The government even refused to let them get married!

Every day they went to get a marriage license. And every day the clerk told them that he had to talk to his boss, and he would let them know tomorrow. Finally he told them that they would never be allowed to marry.

Anatoly was right about Avital's brother; Michael was released after fifteen days in jail. And somehow, a few months later, he received permission to go to Israel. Anatoly and Avital hoped they would soon be able to join him, but they were not so fortunate. One day Anatoly was arrested without a reason. The next day, Avital was called into a governmental office.

"You have been given permission to leave," the official said. "You must leave the country within ten days."

Avital replied that she would not leave without Anatoly.

"If you go now," the official said, "Anatoly will soon be allowed to follow. But if you don't go now, you will never be allowed to leave. You will have to stay here the rest of your lives and we will make things very difficult for both of you."

It was the hardest decision she ever had to make, but in the end Avital decided to leave. She wanted to believe the official's promises. And Anatoly's friends and family told her that she must go.

Anatoly was still in prison. Avital prayed every day that she would see him before she left. If by some miracle Anatoly was released in time, they would get married. Even though Jewish weddings are illegal in the Soviet Union, she had found an old man, a rabbi, to lead the ceremony. She made herself a wedding dress, just in case.

A miracle! Anatoly returned the night before Avital was to leave for Israel. All their friends and relatives gathered in her little apartment. And all night long they sang and danced, while the secret police listened from the hallway.

Avital left for Israel the next morning. That was in 1974. Anatoly was arrested again soon afterwards and in 1978, was charged with being an American spy. He was put in a prison camp under a sentence of hard labor.

For the next eight years, thousands of people throughout the world, both Jews and non-Jews, protested against Anatoly's imprisonment. Due to their efforts he was finally released. In February, 1986, Anatoly and Avital were reunited. They now live in Jerusalem.

QUESTIONS FOR DISCUSSION
- *Why were Avital, Anatoly, and Michael willing to risk their lives to go to Israel?*
- *Why don't all the Jews in the world want to live in Israel?*

The dream of returning to the Jewish homeland

From the day Moses led the Jews out from Egypt to go to the Promised Land, the Jewish homeland has been a central part of Judaism, and living there has been the dream of the Jewish nation.

This Jewish homeland has been referred to, since biblical times, as **Zion**. Love of Zion and the deep desire to return to Zion have always been a strong component of a Jew's life. Anatoly's risking his life in the Soviet Union to go live in Israel is one such example. He understood that the desire to return to Zion has always been the dream of the Jewish people. In his time of deepest trouble, standing before the Soviet court, his last words before being sent to prison were:

> For more than 2,000 years, the Jewish people, my people, have been spread across the earth. But wherever they are, wherever Jews are found, every year they have repeated, "Next Year in Jerusalem." Now, when I am further than ever from my people, from Avital, facing many hard years of imprisonment, I say, turning to my people, my Avital: NEXT YEAR IN JERUSALEM!

What keeps the desire to return to Zion alive in the hearts of Jews?

For nearly two thousand years, most Jews have lived outside of the Jewish homeland, yet they have kept alive the dream of returning. Despite the efforts of many evil rulers to destroy the Jews and their dream, the Jewish people never stopped hoping to return to Zion. The Jews' return to Zion is so important that it is referred to over and over again in the Tanach, prayed for in many *tefillot*, and always referred to in Jewish holiday celebrations.

The Tanach recounts how the Jewish people came into their homeland: from God's promises to Abraham and Moses, to the Jews' wandering in the desert for forty years, and finally, to their crossing of the Jordan River into the Promised Land. Jews read and study these accounts every year as part of the weekly Torah portions. This is one of the many ways in which Jews have remembered their homeland during all the years they lived outside it.

Tefillah is another way in which Jews have kept alive the memory of Zion. Many of the daily *tefillot* refer to the deep desire of the Jewish nation to return to Zion. One typical example in the daily *tefillah* is, "God, please gather us from the four corners of the earth and return us to Zion."

Two thousand years ago, when the Jews lived in Zion, their great temple was in Jerusalem. Today, all that remains of that temple is the Western Wall. Yet, in order to remember Zion and the great temple, Jews to this day, all over the world, face in the direction of the Western Wall in Jerusalem when they pray.

A famous saying also expresses the Jewish love of Zion. At Pesach and Rosh Hashanah, and on other holidays, Jews say "Next Year in Jerusalem!" This phrase has given Jews hope and courage for many centuries, and it still does. Thus, Anatoly Shcharansky ended his reply to his Soviet accusers with these very words, just as other persecuted Jews have done for thousands of years.

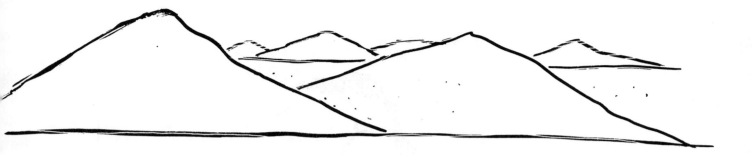

How did love of Zion help the Jews to reestablish their homeland in 1948?

Since the late 1800s, the movement expressing the desire of the Jews to return to their homeland has been called **Zionism**. More than a hundred years ago, Jewish writers and thinkers such as Moses Hess and Achad Ha-Am expressed the idea that Jews should go live in their homeland.

At that time, the area in which the Jewish homeland is located was called Palestine. Palestine, the old Roman name for the area, was never a state or a country. It was, in fact, mostly desert and swamps. Even though very few people lived there, there were always Jewish communities in the land. The only independent states that ever existed there were the two Jewish ones. Since 70 C.E., when the Romans destroyed the second Jewish state and 135 C.E., when the Romans threw the Jews out of their homeland, no other state had ever been established there.

In 1896, Theodor Herzl, the founder of the Zionist movement, wrote a powerful book, entitled *The Jewish State*. This book, as well as books and articles of other Zionist thinkers, inspired thousands of Jews to work to reestablish the Jewish state in their homeland.

In 1897, Herzl organized the First World Zionist Congress in Basle, Switzerland. Hundreds of Jews gathered to discuss how to create a modern Jewish state. As a result, in the early 1900s, many Jewish pioneers went to live in Palestine and within fifty years the Zionist dream became a reality. On May 15, 1948, the modern Jewish state of Israel was created.

Since 1948, more than a million Jews from all over the world have "come home" to Israel. "Returning" to Israel continues to be a Jewish ideal which inspires Jews today to move to Israel. Anatoly Shcharansky's last words before going to prison in 1978 expressed his desire to live in Israel. Anatoly had never seen Israel. Yet his dream of living there kept him alive through all his suffering in Soviet prison camps.

In the land that is known today as Israel, there has never been any independent state except a Jewish one.

Why don't all Jews live in the Jewish state?

It is a difficult thing to leave your own country and settle in a new place. But many Jews have done just that by going to live in Israel, or as it is usually referred to, they have "made **aliyah**." *Aliyah* is a Hebrew word meaning "going up." *Aliyah* is the Torah's term for going up to Jerusalem—the capital of Zion—which is located high up in the mountains. Jews who move to Israel are said to "make *aliyah*." They have "gone up" to Zion.

Throughout Jewish history, Jews have divided the Jewish world into two parts. Israel is one, and outside of Israel, or the **Diaspora**, is the other. For a long time, there were very few Jews in the land of Israel. Almost all the world's Jews lived in the Diaspora. Now there is a Jewish state once again. But most of the world's Jews remain in the Diaspora. Why don't all the Jews in the Diaspora make *aliyah*?

Many Diaspora Jews are satisfied with the lives they have built for themselves and their families. Though they love Israel, they may not wish to live there. Some have lived in their communities for generations and have become well established. Some Jews have even forgotten the dream of returning to Zion.

It is hard to leave family and friends, property and businesses, and go build a new life in a new country. Despite the hardships, however, more than 100,000 North American Jews have made *aliyah* and created successful lives for themselves in Israel. These American Jews are true pioneers, living the Zionist dream and turning it into a reality.

How can Jews in the Diaspora support Israel?

Whether they live in Israel or not, Jews are connected to the State of Israel. Diaspora Jews can do many things to strengthen this connection and to support the Jewish homeland. Israel is a small country surrounded by enemies that wish to destroy it. It has been forced to fight several wars for survival, and at the same time it has absorbed over a million immigrants, most of whom came with nothing but dreams. Israel needs the help and support of Jews everywhere.

One way you can support Israel is to know what is happening there. You can read Jewish and Israeli books, newspapers, and magazines; follow news about Israel on television and radio; and discuss Israel with your parents and teachers. By always being educated about Israel, you will be able to discuss and explain things to others who might not understand Israel's situation or may have been given incorrect information.

You can also support Israel by giving *tzedakah*. Because Israel must put a lot of money towards military defense, it needs help providing hospitals, housing, and other projects important to a developing country.

But the most important way you can support Israel is by spending as much time there as possible. You might visit Israel on your vacation, spend a year or two of your college career there, or spend some time working on a kibbutz. By spending time in Israel, gaining familiarity with its language and way of life, you will strengthen your own personal connection to your homeland.

The most important thing a Jew can do to support Israel is to spend time there.

Is there a conflict when a Jew in the Diaspora Supports Israel?

A Jew who lives in the Diaspora is connected to the Jewish homeland, Israel. This may or may not be a problem, depending on the country where he lives. In countries whose values and ideals are similar to those of Israel, there will be no conflict. In countries whose values and ideals are in opposition to those of Israel, the chances of conflict are great. Here are examples of each of these situations.

The United States

Louis Brandeis, a former Justice of the United States Supreme Court and an active Zionist, pointed out that America's values, based on Judaism, Christianity, and democracy, were very similar to Zionism's values. For example, both Israel and the United States are democracies, have freedom of speech, freedom of religion, value the sanctity of human life, and strongly enforce human rights for their citizens. Therefore, it is not surprising that the United States is the greatest friend of Israel in the world. For all these reasons, Jews and non-Jews in the Unites States can support both countries without conflict.

The Soviet Union

The values of the Soviet Union, on the other hand, are in strong conflict with Israel's values. The Soviet Union is not a democracy, does not allow free speech, free elections, a free press, freedom to worship God, and denies its citizens other basic human rights. In addition, the Soviet Union has been trying to destroy Judaism in that country for over fifty years. It is the chief supplier of political, financial, and military support to those who are trying to destroy Israel.

A Jew in the Soviet Union who supports Israel is living in opposition to the goals and ideals of the Soviet government. This is one reason why Jews who live in the Soviet Union are hated and treated badly. It is also why most Soviet Jews would leave the Soviet Union, if they could. And any Soviet Jew who does express Jewish values and support for Israel lives in fear. At any time he could be arrested and sent to prison.

Anatoly was finally allowed to go to Israel. But there are still thousands of *refuseniks* in the Soviet Union who are risking their lives to return to Zion. As expressed in the words of Israel's national anthem, *Hatikvah*:

As long as a heart beats within
Every Jewish soul is yearning
Looking towards the East.
Our eyes are turning to Zion.

We still have not lost our hope
The hope of 2,000 years
To be a free people in our own land
The land of Zion and Jerusalem.

The powerful dream of Zion is central to Judaism.

chapter 19

Two Booths Are Better Than One

It was the beginning of another day at Golda Meir High School. At exactly 8:30, the principal turned on the PA system and spoke into the microphone.

"Good morning, students," Dr. Dorph said. "I have a special announcement this morning. Most of you know about our city's upcoming carnival. Every group of people living in our city will have a booth there, and the mayor has asked our school to design a booth representing the Jewish community! I'd like to get as many of you involved in this as possible. Anyone interested should come to a meeting after school today, in the auditorium. And for the rest of the day I want all of you to consider the question: what's the best way to represent our Jewish community at the carnival?"

At the after-school meeting, it soon became clear that there were two different answers to Dr. Dorph's question. One group, led by David, put its position this way:

"Since the Jews are a religious group, we should design a booth that displays some of our religious symbols. We could show a Torah, a Siddur, a menorah, a beautiful Passover Haggadah, and an embroidered challah cover. We could place posters next to each object, explaining what it is and how it is used. We want our booth to show Jews as a religious group."

The other group's position was summed up by Susan.

"We think that the Jews are primarily a nation, not a religious group. Jews all over the world feel a connection to each other and to Israel, the Jewish homeland. And because we are a nation, we take care of each other. So we would display posters and photographs of Soviet Jews, Ethiopian Jews, and other Jews who need our help. We also want to put up a big map of Israel with pictures that describe the way of life there. And of course we will show people various Jewish foods. We want our booth to show the Jews as a nation."

The two groups debated for several hours. By now it was close to dinner time, and Dr. Dorph called the meeting to an end.

"Both of the groups have excellent ideas for booths. Unfortunately, we are only allowed to set up one booth and we will not have room for two displays. We'll have to take a vote to decide which booth best represents the Jewish people."

QUESTIONS FOR DISCUSSION
• Which display would you vote for? Why?
• Can you think of another booth that might better represent the Jewish people?

Are the Jews a nation or a religion?

The students at Golda Meir High School proposed two different ideas for a booth. One booth would present the Jews as a religion, the other would present the Jews as a nation. Both of these ideas are right, but neither is totally right. Each booth represents only part of what it means to be Jewish. Being Jewish means being a part of the Jewish religion and the Jewish nation.

Some Jews emphasize the religious part over the national. They might say that the best way to be Jewish is to observe Shabbat and keep kosher. Others identify with the nation rather than the religion. They might believe that supporting Israel and Soviet Jewry is the way to be a good Jew. However, neither the religious nor the national part can stand alone. A good Jew maintains both a religious and national identity.

It is true that there are different groups within Judaism, and that they often have different understandings of parts of Judaism. But they all agree that the Jews are both a nation and a religion.

In this respect, the Jews are unique. There are many nations in the world and there are many religions. But only the Jews are both a nation and a religion.

How Jewish nationality differs from other nationalities

The Jewish nation is the only one in the world that has its own religion. That is why the Jewish nation is the only one in the world that one joins by converting to a religion.

Anyone can become a member of the Jewish nation by converting to Judaism. This is not true about any other nation. To become a member of the nation of the United States, for example, you have to move to and live in the United States—and of course, you can continue to believe in any religion you want. To become a member of the Jewish nation, however, you can continue to live anywhere in the world, but you must undergo a religious conversion to Judaism.

A non-Jewish person who wants to become a member of the Jewish nation must convert to Judaism. A convert becomes a member of the Jewish nation as well as the Jewish religion.

This is illustrated by the story of the first convert in Jewish history, a woman named Ruth. Her story can be found in the Tanach, in the section known as K'tuvim (Writings). Ruth was a non-Jewish woman who married a Jewish man. When her husband died, Ruth decided to stay with Naomi, her Jewish mother-in-law. In some of the most beautiful words of the Bible, she expressed her love for Naomi, for Judaism, and for the Jewish people:

> Where you go, I will go,
> Where you stay, I will stay,
> Your people shall be my people,
> And your God shall be my God.

Ruth used the word "people" to show that she wanted to become part of the Jewish nation. And she spoke of God to show that she wanted to observe the Jewish religion. The first Jewish convert, therefore, became a member of the Jewish religion and the Jewish nation at the same time. Ruth understood that to be a Jew, she had to join both.

Ruth eventually remarried. She had children and grandchildren, and her great-grandson was King David, one of the most beloved and important heroes of Jewish history. Ruth's story shows that a convert becomes as much a part of the Jewish people as anyone born to Jewish parents.

The Jewish nation and religion are one

The Jews will always be *Am Yisrael*, the Jewish nation, the descendants of Abraham, Isaac, and Jacob; and Sarah, Rebecca, Rachel, and Leah. They will forever be united by their belief in God and *mitzvot*, by the Torah, and by Jewish ideals and values.

There will never be a Judaism without the Jewish people to live it and spread its ideals; and there will never be a Jewish people without Judaism to keep it alive and give it its meaning. Judaism cannot survive without the Jewish nation, and the Jewish nation cannot survive without Judaism.

Glossary

For a more detailed explanation of each term, turn to the page number given after its definition.

aliyah going up; usually refers to going to live in Israel. (110)

Am Yisrael the nation or people of Israel; the Jewish people. (100)

atheist someone who does not believe that God exists. (5)

beyn adam l'havero refers to laws that are concerned with relationships between people. (52)

beyn adam la-Makom refers to laws that are concerned with people's relationship to God. (52)

brachah a prayer that blesses God and reminds Jews that God is present in every act. (72)

Diaspora all the places in the world that Jews live outside of Israel. (110)

ethical monotheism the idea that God demands ethical behavior from all people. (5)

Gemarah a section of the Talmud; it contains commentary and explanations of the laws and writings of the Mishnah. (48)

Haftarah the portion of the Nevi'im read every week in synagogue. (46)

kadosh separate or special; on a higher level. (71)

kavannah intention and motivation. (86)

kasher fitting or proper to eat. (90)

kashrut a system that tells Jews what they may or may not eat. (90)

kidushah holiness, closeness to God. (71)

K'tuvim the third section of the Bible. (46)

lashon ha-ra any language or speech that hurts other people. (62)

minyan the minimum of ten people required for certain *tefillot* to take place. (85)

Mishneh Torah a code of Jewish law written by Maimonides. (57)

Mishnah a section of the Talmud; it contains commentary and explanations of the laws found in the Torah. (48)

mitpallel to pray or judge yourself. (82)

mitzvah commandment. (45)

monotheism belief in one God. (4)

Nevi'im the second section of the Bible, consisting of the books of the Prophets. (46)

parasha the portion of the Torah read every week in synagogue. (46)

Shehehiyanu a blessing that is recited at special times in a Jew's life. (84)

shehitah the kosher slaughter of an animal. (93)

Shema the prayer expressing the central Jewish idea that there is one God. (83)

shohet the person who performs a kosher slaughter. (93)

Shulhan Arukh a book which contains one of the major listings of all Jewish law. (57)

Siddur the book which contains the *tefillot*; the prayer book. (83)

Talmud a record of the important discussions about the laws in the Torah that took place between 200 B.C.E. and 500 C.E. (47)

Tanach   the Hebrew word for the Bible. (46)

tefillah   self-judgment; a time for praising God and giving thanks. (82)

Tehillim   the book of Psalms in the K'tuvim section of the Bible. (46)

theist   someone who believes that God exists. (10)

Torah   the first part of the Bible, consisting of the five books of Moses: Genesis, Exodus, Leviticus, Numbers, and Deuteronomy. (46)

tzedakah   an act of justice; specifically refers to giving money or time to those in need. (55)

yetzer ha-ra   the creative force inside a person for doing bad. (32)

yetzer ha-tov   the creative force inside a person for doing good. (32)

Zion   a biblical name for the Jewish homeland. (107)

Zionism   the movement expressing the desire of the Jews to return to their homeland. (109)